MW01533833

Elements of
Electronic Navigation

Elements of
Electronic Navigation

N S Nagaraja

Department of Electrical Communication Engineering
Indian Institute of Science
Bangalore

Tata McGraw-Hill Publishing Company Ltd
New Delhi

This book can be exported from India only by the publishers,
Tata McGraw-Hill Publishing Company Limited

Reprinted 1989

Published by Tata McGraw-Hill Publishing Company Limited, 4/12 Asaf Ali Road, New Delhi,
and printed by Jay Print Pack (Pvt) Ltd, 8/39, Kirti Nagar Industrial Area, New Delhi-110015.

Preface

As IN many other fields, electronics has made a revolutionary impact in the field of navigation. This art which started with the use of a few instruments such as the sextant and the compass followed by the manual calculations has now developed to such an extent that the navigator has at his disposal a vast array of instruments and computers which automatically present his position and the distance he has to travel to his destination and other navigational information. All this has been made possible by the advent of electronics. There are now numerous radio aids to navigation and some aids which do not involve radio emissions of any type but are dependent on electronics for their functioning.

This book aims at giving an introductory treatment of this vast and expanding field. While navigation as such is the field of the professional navigator, the electronic engineer cannot afford to be ignorant of the variety of ways in which the technology of electronics has been applied to navigation. Appropriately then, the subject figures in the syllabus of the bachelor's degree in electronics in most universities. This book is addressed to such an audience.

The emphasis here is on systems and engineering principles rather than details of equipment. Only in a few places are circuits given. Treatment of the details of circuits, etc. are out of place in a book of this nature and size. An attempt has been made to cover most of the important navigational facilities that are in operation in this country and abroad.

A subject such as this where rapid developments are taking place and much of the latest developments are only available in classified literature, any book which deals with details, tends to get obsolete. But a treatment of the basic principles is likely to have a more lasting value.

The book is divided into nine chapters, the first being introductory and the next seven dealing with various common navigational aids including the self-contained systems of Doppler radar and inertial navigation. The last chapter deals briefly with some of the recent developments. Additional matter of relevance is given in the four appendices. A list of references including textbooks is given for further reading on the topics dealt with. As the book is intended for students in the final year of their bachelor's course, a knowledge of basic communication engineering such as is provided by commonly available tests like Terman's *Electronic and Radio Engineering* is assumed. A set of questions and exercises has been included in the end with a view to help the reader increase his appreciation of the subject and to encourage further reading. Metric units of distance have been used throughout the book. As much of the literature on the subject makes use of other units such as the statute mile, nautical mile, knots, etc., the conversion factors are given in a footnote for ready reference.

This book is the result of a suggestion made by Prof S V C Aiya, formerly Head of the Department of Electrical Communication Engineering at the Indian Institute of Science, and the encouragement he gave me.

It has been used in the class room for a number of years and owes its present form to the many helpful suggestions made by the students themselves, for which I thank them. I am also thankful to the Director, Indian Institute of Science, for permitting me to bring out this volume and to Prof B S Ramakrishna, Chairman of Electrical Sciences, for the encouragement he has given. The drawings were prepared by Mr Vijayendra and the manuscript was typed by Mr Govindaraju, and I am grateful to them for the care and trouble they took.

Bangalore,   N S NAGARAJA
26th March, 1975

Contents

Elements of
Electronic Navigation

1

Introduction

1. Introduction

NAVIGATION, the art of directing the movements of a craft from one point to another along a desired path, has an origin going back to pre-historic times. Many great voyages of migration appear to have been undertaken even in the pre-Christian era. In the early days, none of the aids of later navigators, such as the compass, the chronometer and the sextant, were available. These voyages were accomplished perhaps by the voyagers' knowledge of the movements of the sun and the stars and the winds.

As time progressed, various instruments came to the aid of the navigator. By the sixteenth century, the compass, the clock, the theodolite and, at least, crude charts of the known world were available to the navigator. The great navigator, Magellan, circumnavigated the Globe in the early sixteenth century with the aid of these instruments. By the eighteenth century, the chronometer, a very accurate clock, was produced. With the chronometer, the navigator was able to determine his longitude by noting the transit time of heavenly bodies. The other instruments were also improved and the charts became more extensive and accurate. Navigation, by then, had become a science as well as an art. In the twentieth century, electronics entered the field. Time signals were broadcast by which the chronometers could be corrected. Direction finders and other navigational aids which enabled the navigator to obtain a fix using entirely electronic aids were developed and came into extensive use.

Our principal concern in this book is with electronic navigational aids, i.e. navigational systems which employ electronics in some way. However, a brief account of other methods of navigation are included to present the main topic in the proper perspective.

2. Four Methods of Navigation

Navigation requires the determination of the position of the craft and the direction in which it has to go to reach the desired destination. The currently used methods of navigation may be divided into four classes:

(i) Navigation by pilotage (or visual contact),

(ii) Celestial or astronomical navigation,

(iii) Navigation by dead-reckoning, and

(iv) Radio navigation.

We will be concerned with only the last two of these, but, before we proceed, some general ideas regarding the other methods of navigation are desirable.

(i) *Navigation by pilotage.* In this method, the navigator fixes his position on a map by observing known visible landmarks. In air navigation, for example, when the ground is visible, the navigator can see the principal features on the ground, such as rivers, coast-lines, estuaries, hills, etc. and thereby, fix his position. Even at night, light beacons, cities and towns provide information about the position of the craft. Pilotage in this sense is, of course, possible only under conditions of good visibility.

Pilotage is also possible with the aid of an air-borne radar and this is called 'Electronic-Pilotage'. The radar used for this purpose is generally a microwave search radar provided with a plan-position (PPI) display on which the terrain is mapped. The PPI picture has, of course, poor resolution compared with the human eye, because the angular resolution is typically 3° and the resolution radially, along the time-base scan is of the order of a few kilometers. This is, however, sufficient for identifying the more prominent features of the terrain. Electronic pilotage has the advantage that its range is high, generally 50 to 100 km and that it can be used under conditions of poor visibility. In addition, the distance of the objects 'seen' can be determined far more accurately than by visual means. Because of these advantages, radar can be a valuable navigational aid under certain conditions. Both the methods of pilotage require recognizable features in the terrain and would, therefore, be useless over stretches of sea if there are no islands in the field of vision. Both methods of pilotage depend upon the availability of accurate maps of the terrain.

(ii) *Celestial navigation.* Celestial navigation (also called astronomical navigation) is accomplished by measuring the angular position of celestial bodies. Almanacs giving the position of celestial bodies at various times (measured in terms of Greenwich Mean Time) are readily available. The navigator measures the elevation of the celestial body with a sextant and notes the precise time at which the measurement is made with a chronometer. These two measurements are enough to fix the position of the craft on a circle on the face of the globe. If two such observations are made, the position or 'fix' of the craft can be identified as one of the two points of intersections of the circles. If the position of the craft is known approximately, the ambiguity between the two possible positions may be eliminated. Sometimes, a third observation may have to be made to remove the ambiguity.

The basis of this method is as follows. Referring to Fig. 1.1, if P is the position of the craft on the surface of the earth, and Q the point on the surface of

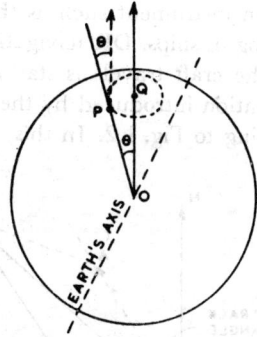

Fig. 1.1
Principle of celestial navigation

the earth at which the celestial body is at the zenith at the time of observation (called the sub-stellar point), the celestial body makes an angle θ with the vertical at P. The arc joining sub-stellar point and the position of the craft also subtends an angle θ at the centre of the earth. The locus of all points subtending this angle is a circle with the sub-stellar point as the centre. The position of the latter can be obtained from the almanac if the exact time of observation is noted. One observation of θ (or the elevation angle $90° - \theta$) gives one position circle. Two observations, providing two intersecting circles, are generally sufficient to obtain a fix. In practice, the two observations are not made at the same instant and consequently the craft will have moved between the instants of observations. But this can be allowed for in the reckoning.

The advantage of celestial navigation is its relative independence of external aids. It has the disadvantage that the visibility should be good enough to take elevation angles of heavenly bodies. This may not be always possible at sea, but in air navigation, with modern aircraft flying at altitudes above 5000 m, visibility is always good.

The accuracy of fixes obtained in this method of navigation depends mainly on the accuracy with which the elevation of the heavenly body is taken. This, in turn, depends on the accuracy with which the horizon can be located. Under favourable conditions, these angles can be measured correct to 1 min of arc, which implies the position line accuracy of one nautical mile.

(iii) *Navigation by dead-reckoning.* In this method of navigation, the position of the craft at any instant of time is calculated from the previously determined position, the speed of its motion with respect to earth along with the direction of its motion (i.e. its velocity vector) and the time elapsed. The term 'dead-reckoning' abbreviated 'DR' stands for 'deduced calculation'*. This is the most common and widely used method of navigation.

---

* The origin of the term is attributed by some to the use of a log attached to the line used in taking measurement of ship's speed at sea. The log is 'dead', i.e. stationary in water while the ship is in motion.

Navigation by dead-reckoning, requires some means of finding the direction of motion of the craft (called the "track angle") and a speed indicator. The first requirement may be met by a magnetic compass and the second by an instrument such as the air-speed indicator in aircraft and the mechanical log in ships. DR navigation would be straight-forward, if the medium in which the craft travels is stationary. But this condition rarely prevails. The complication introduced by the velocity of the medium will be appreciated by referring to Fig. 1.2. In this, the aircraft has a direction of apparent motion, OA,

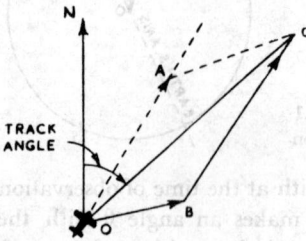

Fig. 1.2
The velocity triangle

which is called the 'heading' of the aircraft. The wind has a velocity in a different direction, OB. The velocity of the aircraft with respect to ground is given by the vector combination of these two, i.e. by OC. The angle which the vector OC makes with the North is called the 'track angle'. It is clear that the heading and track angle are not, in general, the same, the exception being when the wind is in the direction of OA or its reciprocal. Further, the air speed and ground speed are not the same when there is a wind. The true ground speed and direction can, however, be determined by constructing the velocity triangle and DR navigation is, thus possible, if the wind velocity is known. Similar considerations apply to navigation of ships as tidal currents require to be taken into account. But these are known to much better accuracy than wind velocities which keep changing in magnitude and direction constantly. Navigation by dead-reckoning over long distances is subject to appreciable errors unless intermediate checks are possible.

In air navigation, the wind velocity is generally obtained in the course of the flight from weather broadcasts or by communication with ground stations. In long flights over water, modern air operations resort to 'minimal flight paths', i.e. paths which require minimum flying time. If there were no winds, this would be the path of minimum geographical distance, which is the great-circle path between the starting point and the destination. But the presence of winds, particularly high velocity air currents at high altitudes completely alters the situation. The path taking the shortest time uses favourable wind directions and may be longer geographically. If the pattern of isobars ('the pressure pattern') over the region of flight is known, the experienced navigator can take a route which is long geographically but requires shorter time. This is called 'pressure pattern navigation'. The instruments required for this are a barometric altimeter to measure the 'pressure altitude' and a radio altimeter to determine the absolute altitude. The navigator flies at constant pressure altitude and notes the change in absolute altitude over an interval of time. With this information, he is able to compute the cross-component of the wind which is required for dead-reckoning, and serves as a check on predicted pressure and wind. (For further details of this method, see Ref. 3).

In recent years, new techniques of determining the true velocity and direction of motion have been developed. These employ sensors of acceleration based on inertial principles and sensors of velocity based on Doppler effect and have given rise to 'Inertial navigation' and 'Doppler navigation' respectively. The principles of these methods are the subject of Chapters 7 and 8.

(iv) *Radio navigation.* This method is based on the use of electromagnetic waves to find the position of the craft. The various techniques employed form the subject matter of the greater part of the following chapters where a number of common systems are described. All these systems depend upon transmitters and/or receivers at known locations on the earth's surface and transmitters and/or receivers working in conjunction with them in the vehicle. These systems involve a dependence of the craft on installations on land and are, therefore, not self-contained systems of navigation like the DR system. In the last analysis, all these systems depend on the properties of rectilinear propagation and constant velocity of electromagnetic waves and the navigational parameters (direction, distance, etc.) are obtained by direct or indirect measurement of delay (or delays) occurring in the transmission. The positional information is related principally to (i) the measurement of direction, (ii) the measurement of distance, or (iii) the difference in distance of two transmitters. These give the locus of the craft on (i) a line, (ii) a circle, and (iii) a hyperbola, respectively. The intersection of two or more such loci gives the fix or position of the craft.

In the following chapters the principles underlying a number of such systems are discussed.

2

Radio Direction-finding

THE earliest method of electronic navigation was by direction-finding, i.e. the determination of the direction of arrival of electromagnetic waves at the receiving station. As electromagnetic waves travel along the great-circle path, direction-finding helps to locate the transmitter along a great circle. Though the oldest form of electronic navigation, this method is still in wide use both on ships and aircraft.

The direction-finder may be located either on the craft or on ground. In the former case, the determination of the bearing of two or more fixed stations will give a 'fix'. In the latter case, the ground station finds the bearing of the craft and passes on the information to the craft by a radio communication channel. Both the methods are in vogue.

Direction-finding may be carried out in any region of the radio spectrum, though certain frequencies are specifically allotted for navigational purposes, in the LF/MF, HF and VHF bands. The technical features of direction finders operating at these frequencies naturally differ, but the fundamental principles involved are the same. These will be considered next, with the loop antenna (which is used mainly at low and medium frequencies) as the basis.

2.1 The Loop Antenna

Consider a rectangular loop antenna of length a and width b (Fig. 2.1) with its plane vertical, mounted so that it can be rotated about the vertical axis. Let there be a vertically polarized electromagnetic wave incident on it, coming from a direction making an angle θ with the plane of the loop*. The

---

* In all the following discussions, it will be assumed that the direction of the incoming wave is fixed, i.e. from the East. The polar diagram is, therefore, interpreted as the polar plot of the loop output when the loop is rotated about its axis.

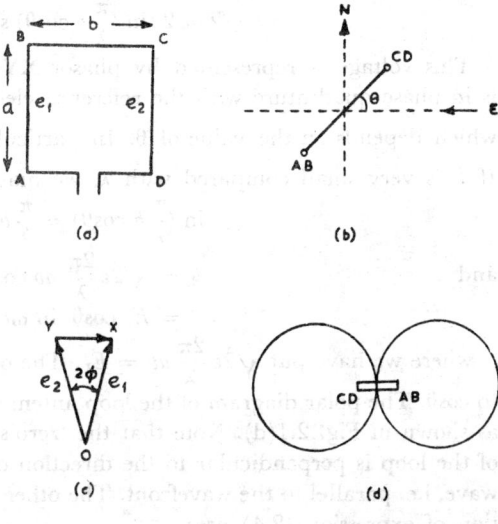

Fig. 2.1
(a) Loop antenna, (b) its setting, (c) phasor diagram and (d) polar diagram

source will be assumed to be so far away, that the incident wave is a plane wave. Voltages are induced in the vertical members of the loop, but not in its horizontal members as the wave is vertically polarized. The magnitude of the voltage induced in the two vertical members is $a \cdot \varepsilon$ where ε is the magnitude (say rms) of the electric field. The voltages in the two members will not be in phase, as can be seen in the phasor diagram, Fig. 2.1(c). Taking the electric field at the centre of the loop as the reference, the voltage induced in AB [represented by phasor OX in Fig. 2.1(c)] lags by an angle ϕ and that induced in CD leads by an equal angle. The difference in path lengths being $\frac{1}{2}b \cos\theta$, the phase difference ϕ is given by

$$\phi = \frac{2\pi}{\lambda} \tfrac{1}{2} b \cos\theta$$

$$= \frac{\pi}{\lambda} b \cos\theta \qquad (2.1)$$

If the electric field at the centre of the loop is

$$\varepsilon(t) = \sqrt{2}\, \varepsilon \cos(\omega t)$$

the voltages induced in AB and CD are then

$$e_1 = \sqrt{2}\, a\varepsilon \cos\left(\omega t - \frac{\pi}{\lambda} b \cos\theta\right)$$

and

$$e_2 = \sqrt{2}\, a\varepsilon \cos\left(\omega t + \frac{\pi}{\lambda} b \cos\theta\right)$$

$$(2.2)$$

The resultant voltage around the loop is thus

$$e_{\mathrm{L}} = e_1 - e_2 = 2a\varepsilon \cos\left(\omega t - \frac{\pi}{\lambda} b \cos\theta\right) - \cos\left(\omega t + \frac{\pi}{\lambda} b \cos\theta\right)$$

$$= \sqrt{2}\, a\varepsilon\, 2 \sin \left(\frac{\pi}{\lambda}\, b \cos\theta\right) \sin \omega t \qquad (2.3)$$

This voltage is represented by phasor XY in Fig. 2.1(c). The voltage e_L is in phase quadrature with the reference electric field and has a magnitude which depends on the value of θ. In particular, when θ is $\frac{\pi}{2}$ or $\frac{3\pi}{2}$, $e_L = 0$. If b is very small compared with λ, we may put

$$\sin \left(\frac{\pi}{\lambda}\, b \cos\theta\right) \approx \frac{\pi}{\lambda}\, b \cos\theta$$

and

$$e_L = \sqrt{2}\varepsilon \frac{2\pi}{\lambda}\, ab \cos\theta \sin \omega t$$

$$= E_L \cos\theta \sin \omega t \qquad (2.4)$$

where we have put $\sqrt{2}\varepsilon \frac{2\pi}{\lambda}\, ab = E_L$. The output amplitude is proportional to $\cos\theta$. The polar diagram of the loop antenna is, therefore, a 'figure-of-eight' as shown in Fig. 2.1(d). Note that the 'zero's or nulls occur when the plane of the loop is perpendicular to the direction of arrival of the electromagnetic wave, i.e. parallel to the wavefront. The other points that emerge on examination of expression (2.4) are:

(a) The output voltage is proportional to the area of the loop, ab.

(b) The phase of the output voltage reverses when loop passes through a null, i.e. if in one lobe of the figure-of-eight it is leading the reference field by $\pi/2$, then in the other lobe it lags the reference field by $\pi/2$.

If the loop has N turns instead of one, the output voltages of the turns add up and the resulting output is N times that of a single turn loop. In the above discussion, we have considered a rectangular loop, but the conclusions are applicable to loops of other shapes (e.g. triangular or circular ones) because these may be considered as made up of an infinite number of elementary rectangular loops, for each of which the output voltage is proportional to the area. As a consequence, the loop voltage is proportional to the loop area, irrespective of the shape of the loop.

In the above analysis, we have obtained the voltage output of the loop from the electric field of the incoming wave. Precisely the same results are obtained if we calculate the voltage on the basis of the magnetic field. The output in this case, will depend on the rate of change of magnetic flux linked with the loop. When the loop is East-West, the linkage is maximum and the output is, likewise, maximum. When the loop is North-South, its plane is parallel to the wave front and there is no flux linkage. The output is, therefore, zero.

The markedly directional property of the loop antenna can be used for direction-finding. The procedure consists in feeding the loop antenna output to a receiver, and turning the loop until a null is obtained. The direction of arrival of the electromagnetic wave is then determined (with an ambiguity of 180°) as the one normal to the plane of the loop. The null, rather than the maximum signal is chosen because it is more sharply defined, i.e. at the null, the rate of change of signal with angular displacement of the loop is higher than at the maximum of the figure-of-eight.

The ambiguity of 180° arises because, the two nulls are indistinguishable from each other when only the magnitude of the signal is considered. But the nulls are distinguishable when the phase of the signal is also considered. For example, if the loop is turned clockwise, at one null the phase of the signal (with respect to the reference field) changes from $\pi/2$ leading to $\pi/2$ lagging, and at the other null, it changes from $\pi/2$ lagging to $\pi/2$ leading. Therefore, some method of finding the phase of the signal with respect to the reference field can be used for resolving the ambiguity. This process is called 'sense-finding'.

For sense-finding, a vertical antenna is used in conjunction with the loop. The vertical antenna is non-directional (i.e. its horizontal polar diagram is circular) and it is kept close to the loop antenna so that the voltage induced in it is in phase with the reference field. The output voltages of the vertical antenna and the loop antenna are then respectively

$$\left. \begin{aligned} e_V &= K \cos\omega t \\ e_L &= \cos\theta \sin\omega t \end{aligned} \right\} \tag{2.5}$$

omitting some constants of proportionality. The factor K is the ratio of the vertical antenna output amplitude to the maximum loop antenna output amplitude. These two voltages are in phase quadrature, as is also evident from the phasor diagram in Fig. 2.1(c). If the phase of one of them is changed by 90° and the two voltages are then added, sense-finding is possible because the voltage from the loop will add to or subtract from that of the sense aerial depending on the direction of arrival of the electromagnetic wave. Let us assume that the phase of the loop output is changed by $\pi/2$ making it

$$e'_L = \cos\theta \cos\omega t$$

The sum of the two voltages, which is the input to the receiver E is given by

$$E_i = K \cos\omega t + \cos\theta \cos\omega t$$
$$= (K + \cos\theta) \cos\omega t \tag{2.6}$$

Thus when $\theta = 0$, the amplitude of the input is $(K + 1)$ and when $\theta = \pi$, it is $(K - 1)$. If E_i is plotted as a function of θ, we get the polar diagram of the combined antenna. These plots are shown in Fig. 2.2 for several values of K. Ideally, K should be unity, giving the cardioid pattern [Fig. 2.2(c)] in which

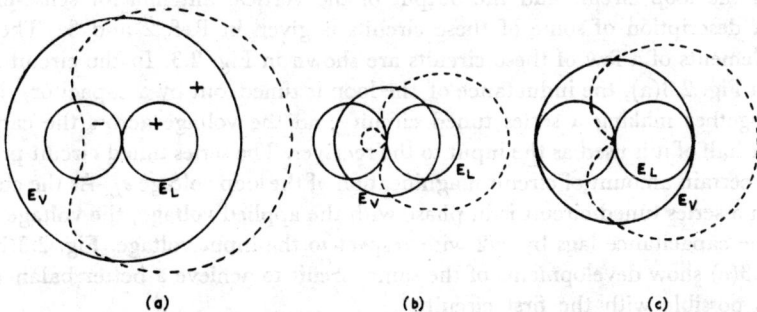

Fig. 2.2 Polar diagrams of combined vertical antenna and loop antenna (a) $K > 1$, (b) $K < 1$, and (c) $K = 1$

the correct direction of the wave and its reciprocal are distinguished by a large difference in the combined output. It should be noted, however, that while for direction-finding the loop is turned to give zero or minimum signal, for sense-finding, it should be turned to give the maximum loop signal. The procedure for direction-finding consists, then, of the following steps: (a) with the sense antenna disconnected, the loop is turned to give the minimum signal and its angular position is noted; (b) then the loop is turned clockwise (say) by 90°. The signal increases to its maximum; (c) the sense antenna is now connected. If the orientation of the loop indicates the correct direction, the signal increases and if it indicates the reciprocal, the signal decreases. (Note that two conventions have been introduced in this procedure—firstly that the loop is turned *clockwise* after obtaining the null and secondly that the signal *increases* when the correct direction is indicated. In order that this may be true, appropriate connections of the loop terminals have to be made).

In loop antennas, an undesirable effect known as the 'antenna effect' arises due to the pick-up of a small voltage (either in the receiver or elsewhere) which is independent of the orientation of the loop. The loop antenna is used to find the zero signal position, and, therefore, even a very small extraneous voltage adversely affects the operation. If the pick-up voltage is in phase-quadrature to the voltage around the loop, it merely changes the null to a minimum and broadens it ('*quadrature antenna effect*'). If it is in phase with the loop output voltage, it makes the two lobes of the figure-of-eight pattern unequal, as in Fig. 2.2(b) ($K < 1$). The most important change brought about in this case is the non-opposite nature of the two minima, which can be readily checked in practice.

2.2   Loop Input Circuits

The loop antenna is by itself inductive and the loop output is not generally used directly as an input to the receiver. A variety of circuits is used at the input of direction-finding receivers to obtain a voltage which is larger than the loop voltage and to establish the desired phase relation between the output of the loop circuit and the output of the vertical antenna for sense-finding. A description of some of these circuits is given in Ref. 2 and 3. The basic elements of a few of these circuits are shown in Fig. 2.3. In the circuit shown in Fig. 2.3(a), the inductance of the loop is tuned out by a capacitor, the two together making a series tuned circuit, and the voltage across the capacitor or half of it is used as the input to the receiver. The series tuned circuit provides a certain amount of circuit magnification of the loop voltage e_L. As the currrent in a series tuned circuit is in phase with the applied voltage, the voltage across the capacitance lags by $\pi/2$ with respect to the input voltage. Fig. 2.3(b) and 2.3(c) show developments of the same circuit to achieve a better balance than is possible with the first circuit.

One of the important sources of antenna effect is the asymmetry of the loop antenna with respect to the ground. To minimize antenna effect, the centre

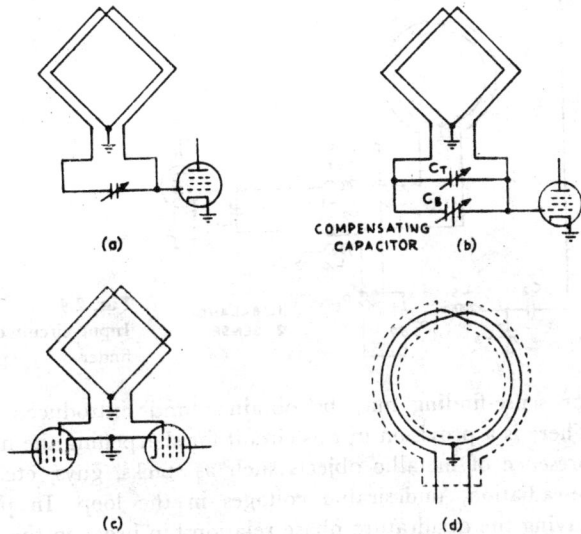

Fig. 2.3 Loop input circuits: (a) series tuned; (b) & (c) balanced circuits; (d) a screened loop

of the loop is earthed and its output is, thereby, balanced. If the input stage of the receiver is single-ended, half the voltage across the tuning capacitor is applied to the grid of the first stage and some unbalance may be introduced by the input capacitance. To remove such an unbalance, either a compensating capacitor C_B may be used as in Fig. 2.3(b) or a balanced input stage may be employed as in Fig. 2.3(c). Any residual antenna effect can be compensated by introducing a controllable voltage in phase with the antenna voltage. In all adjustments aimed at eliminating antenna effect, a check is made to see whether the minima correspond to opposite bearings by tuning in a station and turning the loop. Ideally, the two bearings obtained must differ by 180° and any departure from this figure is minimized by adjustment of the compensating circuits.

Balancing of the loop is made more effective and accurate by enclosing it in an electrostatic shield which is broken at one point near the top. A completely shielded loop will, of course, not pick up any signal but if a break is introduced, the performance of the loop is scarcely affected, while any unbalance introduced by surrounding objects is minimized. The receiver can be an ordinary communications receiver but with arrangement for switching off automatic volume control.

2.3 An Aural-Null Direction-Finder

The input circuit of a manually operated loop direction-finder is shown in Fig. 2.4. This circuit illustrates one method by which the voltage required

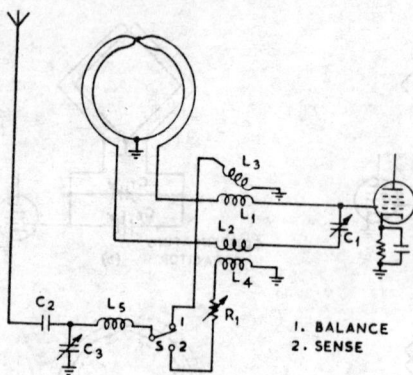

1. BALANCE
2. SENSE

Fig. 2.4

Input circuit of an aural-null direction-finder

for sense-finding may be obtained and introduced into the loop circuit. There is a provision in this circuit for sharpening the nulls. On shipboard, the presence of metallic objects such as stacks, guys, etc. tends to produce, by re-radiation, undesirable voltages in the loop. In particular, the voltages having the quadrature phase relationship broaden the null. Provision is made in this circuit to introduce a quadrature voltage which can be adjusted to cancel the picked-up voltage. The operation of the circuit is as follows.

The loop circuit consisting of the loop antenna, L_1, C_1 and L_2 is a series tuned circuit for the loop voltage. In the 'Balance' position of switch S, an additional voltage is introduced through the variable inductive coupling between L_3 and L_1. This voltage is obtained from the vertical antenna and the components C_2, L_5 and C_3 are so adjusted that this voltage is in phase quadrature to the loop voltage. With the variation in magnitude and sign permitted by the variable coupling between L_1 and L_3, the quadrature component arising from 'antenna effect' can be cancelled out. For sense finding, the switch S is thrown to position 2. The vertical antenna circuit has now a large series resistance R_1. The current in L_4 is, therefore, in phase with the vertical antenna voltage and the voltage induced in L_2 is in phase quadrature to this, i.e. it is either in phase or in phase opposition to the loop voltage. This satisfies the requirement for sense finding. The magnitude of this voltage can be adjusted to the optimum value to get good sense discrimination by adjusting the resistance R_1. The direction-finding procedure consists of the following steps: with the switch S in position 'Balance', the bilateral bearing of the signal source is found, using, if necessary, the coil L_3 to sharpen the null. The loop is then turned by 90° and the switch is thrown to the 'sense' position. Then by noting whether the signal strength increases or decreases, the sense can be determined. To facilitate sense-finding, the direction-finders have two scales, one for bearing and the second one for sense, the latter being displaced with respect to the former by 90°. To turn the antenna by 90°, therefore, the pointer on the direction-finding scale is turned to the same numerical value on the sense-finding scale.

2.4 The Goniometer

The loop direction-finder has the disadvantage that the loop has to be small enough to be rotated easily. This results in relatively small signal pick-ups. Further, to facilitate manual operation, the loop has to be located near the receiver. This is a requirement which is not always easy to meet, particularly on ship-board. Both these disadvantages are eliminated by using two fixed loops, mutually perpendicular, and combining their outputs in a 'goniometer'. The loops, being fixed, can be as large as practicable and the goniometer can be placed along with the receiver in any convenient location. The antenna and goniometer arrangement is shown in Fig. 2.5.

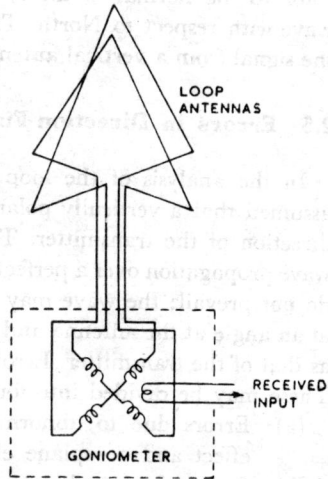

LOOP
ANTENNAS

RECEIVED
INPUT

GONIOMETER

Fig. 2.5
Sketch of the goniometer

The goniometer consists of two windings, mutually perpendicular (called the 'stators'), and a winding at the centre of these, called the 'rotor', which can be rotated about the axis of symmetry. The two fixed loops are connected to the two stator windings and the voltage induced in the rotor is taken to the receiver. It will be shown in the following paragraph that the voltage induced in the rotor is equivalent to the voltage in a rotating loop antenna.

Referring to Fig. 2.6(a), let the two loops be oriented N-S and E-W and let the incident electromagnetic wave (vertically polarized) make an angle θ with the North. The currents flowing in the two loops are then proportional to $\cos\theta$ (N-S loop) and $\cos(90 - \theta) = \sin\theta$ (E-W loop). For convenience, let the corresponding stator coils be called N-S coil and E-W coil. The magnetic flux in these coils, produced by the loop currents are proportional to $\cos\theta$ and $\sin\theta$ respectively [Fig. 2.6(b)], and the resultant magnetic flux has the same direction with respect to the N-S stator that the electromagnetic wave has with respect to the normal to the N-S loop. The voltage induced in the rotor is maximum when the flux is perpendicular to the plane of the rotor and

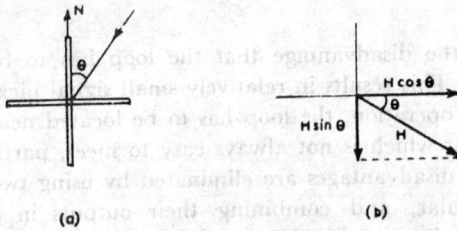

(a) Plan of the loop antennas, and
(b) the magnetic field within the
goniometer

zero when it is parallel to the plane of the rotor. The bearing can be found
by turning the rotor to a null, and taking the direction of the plane of the
rotor to the normal to the N-S stator coil as the direction of the incoming
wave with respect to North. The signal from the rotor can be combined with
the signal from a vertical antenna for sense finding.

2.5   Errors in Direction-Finding

In the analysis of the loop direction-finder given in Sec. 2.1, we have
assumed that a vertically polarized wave is arriving at the antenna from the
direction of the transmitter. This condition will hold good only for ground-
wave propagation over a perfectly conducting earth. In practice such conditions
do not prevail; the wave may not be normally polarized, it may be incident
at an angle at the antenna and the direction of its arrival may not be the same
as that of the transmitter. Errors will arise in direction-finders on this account.
These may be divided into four broad classes as given below.

(a) Errors due to abnormal polarization of the incoming wave (night
effect and aeroplane effect).
(b) Errors due to abnormal propagation.
(c) Site errors, arising from re-radiation of energy from neighbouring
objects.
(d) Instrumental errors, arising from imperfections of the receiving
apparatus.

These will be considered in turn.

(a)   Polarization Errors

In the early days of direction-finding, a type of error was observed, mainly
at night time, which was characterized by displaced minima, rapid changes
in their position, a poor null, etc. The cause of this proved to be the abnormal
polarization associated with ionospheric propagation. As sky-waves were
more prominent at night in the low frequency band, the name 'night effect'
was given to this phenomenon. However, at high frequencies, it may occur
at all times of the day. Abnormal polarization also occurs in radiation from
aircraft transmitters and the so-called 'aeroplane effect' has, therefore, the
same basic origin as night-effect.

Consider a loop antenna set to receive an electromagnetic wave incident at an angle β measured from the vertical (Fig. 2.7). Let the polarization be

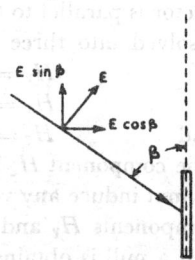

Fig. 2.7

Sketch of normally polarized wave incident on loop antenna

vertical, i.e. let the electric vector be in the vertical plane in the direction of propagation. The emf induced in the loop may be regarded as the sum of those due to two components of the electric vector E, a vertical component $E \sin\beta$ and a horizontal component $E \cos\beta$ in the plane of propagation of the incoming wave. If the loop is positioned with its plane at right angles to the plane of propagation, the net voltage developed in the loop due to the vertical component is zero, and the horizontal component does not induce a voltage in any part of the loop at all. Therefore, a null is obtained in the correct direction and no error will result. An electromagnetic wave polarized in this way is said to be 'normally polarized'.

Consider now a plane polarized wave incident at an angle β but with the electric vector making an angle α with the vertical. This situation is represented in Fig. 2.8(a), where cartesian coordinate axes have been drawn.

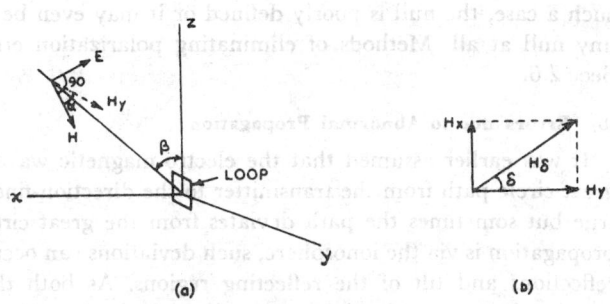

(a)   (b)

Fig. 2.8 (a) Sketch of abnormally polarized wave incident on loop antenna and (b) components of the magnetic field inducing the loop voltage

The direction of propagation is in the XZ plane and the loop can be rotated about the Z-axis. If the loop is positioned in the YZ plane, a null is not obtained as with normally polarized wave because there is a Y-component of the electric field which will induce voltages in the horizontal members of the loop. A null is obtained away from this position. It is easier in this case to analyze the behaviour of the loop with reference to the magnetic vector

H, noting that the voltage induced in the loop is proportional to the magnetic vector normal to the loop and that no voltage is induced if the magnetic vector is parallel to the loop. The H-vector of the plane-polarized wave can be resolved into three components.

$$\left.\begin{array}{l} H_y = H\cos\alpha \text{ along the } y\text{-axis} \\ H_x = H\sin\alpha \ \cos\beta \text{ along the } x\text{-axis} \\ H_z = H\sin\alpha \ \sin\beta \text{ along the } z\text{-axis} \end{array}\right\} \qquad (2.7)$$

and

The component H_z has no effect as it is parallel to the plane of the loop and cannot induce any voltage in it, whatever the orientation of the loop. The two components H_y and H_x, being in time phase, produce a resultant field $H\delta$, and a null is obtained if the loop is turned by an angle δ such that its plane is parallel to $H\delta$ instead of H_x as with a normally polarized wave. By simple trigonometry [Fig. 2.8(b)],

$$\tan\delta = \tan\alpha.\cos\beta \qquad (2.8)$$

The bearing obtained is in error by the angle δ, which is a function of both the angle of incidence (β) and the polarization angle α. For purposes of comparison of different direction-finders, a 'standard wave' is specified, having $\alpha = \beta = \pi/4$. The error δ obtained with this wave is called the 'standard wave error'. For the loop aerial which has been studied, this is, from Eq. 2.8, $\tan^{-1} 1/\sqrt{2}$, i.e. approximately 35.5°.

In the above simple analysis, only the effect of the incident wave is considered and the wave reflected by the ground has been ignored. This will not lead to a serious error as the effect of the reflected wave is generally small.

Sometimes the down-coming wave is not plane-polarized and the various voltages induced in the loop by the components are not in time phase. In such a case, the null is poorly defined or it may even be impossible to obtain any null at all. Methods of eliminating polarization errors are discussed in Sec. 2.6.

(b) Errors due to Abnormal Propagation

It was earlier assumed that the electro-magnetic wave travelled along the great circle path from the transmitter to the direction-finder. This is generally true but sometimes the path deviates from the great circle plane. When the propagation is via the ionosphere, such deviations can occur owing to scattered reflections and tilt of the reflecting regions. As both these phenomena are associated with propagation via the ionosphere, they are more evident at high frequencies. Errors arising from these causes are random and can be specified only in terms of the rms value, which appears to be about 1° (Ref. 4).

Abnormal propagation can also occur at low and medium frequencies under certain conditions. When the direction-finder is near a coast and the direction of arrival of the wave makes a small angle with the coast-line, there is a bending of the wave towards the land owing to the differences in the conductivity of the sea and land. The transmitter, therefore, appears to be more towards the sea than it actually is. This phenomenon is sometimes called 'coastal refraction'. These errors are generally small (about 1°) and generally constant and could be corrected by calibration. A similar phenomenon may be observed in mountainous terrain, owing to the tendency of the electro-magnetic wave to travel along valleys. In air-borne direction-finders, moun-tainous terrain may cause errors when there is a simultaneous reception of the signal from the transmitter by a direct path and by reflection from a mountain side. This is called 'mountain effect'. When it is present, the apparent direction indicated by the direction-finder shows irregular fluctuations about the true course.

(c) **Site Errors**

An ideal site for a direction-finder must be flat (i.e. without any obstacles) and must have a high conductivity. In actual sites, these conditions are not fulfilled and errors arise either on account of reflections from large surfaces or on account of re-radiation from various objects nearby. Even objects underground, such as buried cables, pipes, etc. can produce errors because the soil conductivity is low and the electromagnetic wave penetrates the soil to some depth. It is difficult to assess the effect of nearby objects with any certainty but as a broad generalization it may be said that larger the object and nearer it is to the direction-finder, the greater is its potentiality for intro-ducing site errors. A full discussion of the problems of siting direction-finders may be found in Ref. 5.

In a mobile installation, as on a shipboard, the choice of site is very restricted and the direction-finder is invariably surrounded by objects which absorb some of the energy from the wave and re-radiate it. These cases merit separate study both in view of their special features and of their importance.

On shipboard, metallic objects such as stacks, poles, guys and rigs act as 're-radiators'. This last term is used in a broad sense as the fields produced by these objects at the direction-finder antenna are not necessarily radiation fields, but include induction fields, both magnetic and electrostatic. If the antenna is on the centre-line of the ship, the errors tend to be zero in four directions, namely forward, astern, and to either side. The plot of error versus the bearing of the transmitter appears as shown in Fig. 2.9, and the error is called 'quadrantal error' as it is maximum in each of the four quadrants. The sign of the quadrantal error is such that the apparent bearings tend to be shifted towards the forward or stern part of the ship. The reason for the quandrantal nature of the error is that the large errors are introduced by the loop structures on the ship, made up of mast and hull or stack, which are aligned roughly fore and aft. The loop antenna has maximum coupling with these when its plane is also fore and aft. and minimum coupling when its plane is turned by 90°. When a transmitter is along the centre-line of the ship, the loop structure of the ship has maximum induced currents, but these do not induce any voltage in the loop antenna when the latter is turned to obtain a null, for it will then be at right angles to the centre-line and will have mini-mum coupling to the loop structure. The error is, therefore, zero or minimum. When the transmitter is at right angles to the centre-line of the ship, the loop

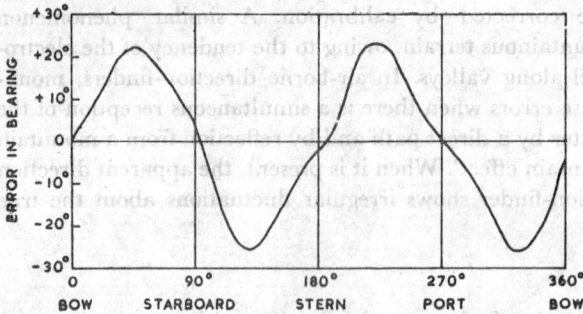

Fig. 2.9 Quadrantal error curve of a ship-board direction-finder

structure has nett zero voltage induced in it and will, therefore, not affect the loop antenna minimum. The error is thus again zero or minimum. Between these four positions, the error is maximum and the nulls may also be poor, requiring balancer adjustments. In addition to the loop structure, some vertical members may re-radiate and give rise to 'semi-circular errors', i.e. errors which are maximum at two points on the circle. These errors, which are of the nature of 'antenna effect' can generally be compensated by balancer adjustments.

The loop structure of the greatest importance is the mast-stack combination making up an open loop. The errors arising from this can be compensated largely by closing the loop by a "compensator"[6] which consists of one or more conductors stretched besween the mass and the stack. Shielding the loop, as stated earlier, also helps to reduce the errors arising from open radiators. In spite of all these precautions and compensations, the residual errors in ship-borne direction-finders are appreciable and calibration is essential. In some installations, mechanical means of automatically applying the correction are incorporated.

Quadrantal error occurs in aircraft direction-finders also, owing to the distortion in the field pattern produced by the wings, engines, propellers and other parts of the aircraft. Airborne direction-finders are almost always provided with cam mechanisms, by which corrections are automatically applied.

(d) Instrumental Errors

Errors also arise owing to imperfections of the components used in direction-finders. In manually operated ones, the most important is the octantal error introduced by the goniometer. In automatic direction-finders, other components such as synchros, resolvers, etc. may also introduce errors. All these errors are generally small and if required could be compensated by calibration.

2.6 Adcock Direction-Finders

It was shown in the last section that polarization errors arise owing to the voltage picked up by the horizontal members of the loop. The Adcock antenna is designed to eliminate polarization errors by dispensing with the horizontal members. It consists of a pair or more of vertical antennas, the signals from these being taken to the receiver either by underground conductors or by shielded balanced pair of wires. In the first case, no voltage will be induced in the horizontal member, if the conductivity of the earth is good, and in the second case, whatever voltages are induced in the two horizontal members tend to cancel out. Several forms of the Adcock antenna are shown in Fig. 2.10. These are generally called U-type or H-type Adcock antennas, depending on the position of the horizontal members, relative to the vertical members.

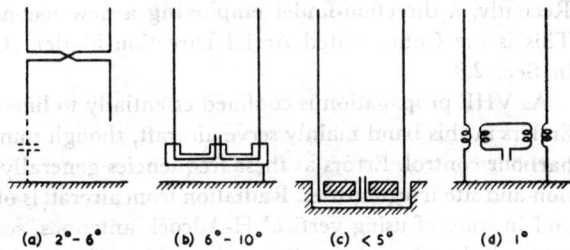

(a) 2°- 6°   (b) 6°- 10°   (c) < 5°   (d) 1°

Fig. 2.10 Adcock direction finders (the standard-wave error is indicated in each case)

Electrically, the Adcock antenna is equivalent to a single-turn loop, and, therefore, for equal sized ones, the output of the former is very low. To compensate for this, the vertical antennas are made large and consequently, a fixed antenna system in conjunction with a goniometer is employed at the low, medium and high frequencies. The need for large antennas also makes the Adcock direction-finder unsuitable for mobile installations. Another disadvantage of this type of antenna is that it has a high internal impedance which is largely capacitive and presents some difficulties in connecting it to the input circuits of a receiver[6]. Sense-finding in the Adcock antenna system is carried out in the same manner as in the loop system, by using a vertical antenna.

The Adcock direction-finder is not completely free from polarization errors, because some voltage is induced in the horizontal members even when buried underground. The errors are, however, reduced. Typical values are also indicated in Fig. 2.10. In antennas of the type shown in Fig. 2.10(a) which are used commonly in the VHF band, errors can arise due to unequal capacitances between the antenna and the earth, but they become less as the height of the antenna system above the earth is increased.

2.7 Direction-Finding at Very High Frequencies

Direction-finding in the frequency band 100-150 MHz is widely employed for aeronautical navigation purposes. This is done by ground-based installations, which obtain the aircraft bearing and pass it to the aircraft by radio telephony. Adcock direction-finders are invariably used for this purpose. In the VHF band, the size of the vertical antenna and its spacing are such that the complete antenna system can be easily rotated. A typical manually operated installation consists of a rotatable aerial system mounted on a mast above the direction-finder (DF) hut with the receiver in the hut. Modern direction-finders are commonly of the automatic type and use a crossed-H Adcock antenna with a capacitor goniometer. The principles of operation of a 'phase-comparison' direction-finder are given in Sec. 2.8. An alternative type, employing modulation techniques, is described in Ref. 4 and 7. Recently, a direction-finder employing a new technique has been developed. This is the Commutated Aerial Direction-Finder (CADF) and is dealt with in Sec. 2.9.

As VHF propagation is confined essentially to line-of-sight ranges, direction-finders in this band mainly serve aircraft, though some use is made of them for harbour control. Errors at these frequencies generally originate from polarization and site irregularities. Radiation from aircraft is often abnormally polarized and in spite of using vertical H-Adcock antennas, some error will be present, particularly when the radiation is incident from a high angle. Site errors are more prominent when the radiation arrives at a low angle and in this case, the choice of a good site is important.

2.8   Automatic Direction-Finders

Manually-operated direction-finders have the virtue of relative simplicity and the advantages associated with a human operator who can exercise the faculty of auditory discrimination in the presence of interfering signals. But in many situations, the need for an operator and the slowness inherent in manual operation are serious disadvantages. An obvious example is that of a direction-finder in an aircraft, where the aircrew is fully occupied with other tasks and carrying an additional crew member is uneconomical. Another instance is where the ground direction-finder has to take the bearing of an aircraft and pass on the information to the control tower. An automatic direction-finder which can give a remote indication at the control tower has distinct advantages in this situation. Automatic direction-finders of many types have been developed to meet such requirements[2,4,7,10]. Here, only two such systems will be described, namely the radio compass, an air-borne direction-finder operating in the LF/MF band (200-3000 kc/s) and the ground-based automatic direction-finder operating in the VHF band.

(a)   The Radio Compass

The radio compass uses a loop antenna in a servo feed-back system. The loop antenna is coupled to the servo-motor which is actuated by an error signal derived from the loop output and turns the loop until the error signal and, therefore, the loop output is zero. It thus automatically positions the loop to a null. For the proper operation of the system, the error signal must change its sign as it passes through zero and to achieve this, an arrangement equivalent to a phase sensitive detector is used. As pointed out in (b) in the analysis of Eq. 2.4, the phase of the carrier undergoes a reversal on passing through zero and the error signal will correspondingly change its sign if a phase sensitive detector is used. This arrangement still permits two positions of equilibria corresponding to the two nulls but one of them is unstable. The loop, therefore, takes up only one position in these circumstances.

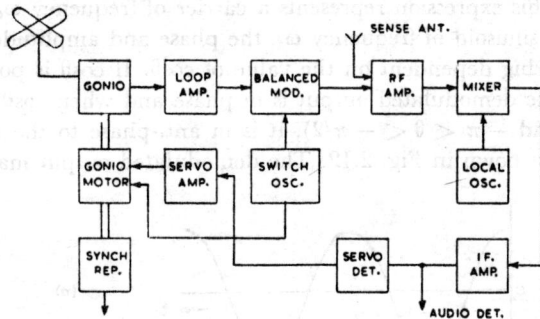

Fig. 2.11 Block diagram of a radio compass receiver

A block-diagram of the radio compass is shown in Fig. 2.11. The equipment is provided with a pair of fixed loops and a gonio which is mechanically coupled to a motor and a synchro-generator. The motor is a two-phase one, actuated by two inputs—one from the switching oscillator and the other from the receiver output. The former is a constant input and, therefore, provides a fixed reference and the latter, a signal in phase with this or exactly 180° out of phase, depending on the position of the loop with respect to the direction of arrival of the signal. The direction of the torque on the motor correspondingly changes its sign depending on the position of the loop and the motor tends to move the gonio to the position of zero torque or the null.

To obtain an output which is dependent on the phase of the gonio signal, the following method is employed. The output of the gonio is fed to a balanced modulator and modulated by a signal from the switching oscillator. The output of the balanced modulator, which consists only of the side band components, is combined with the sense aerial input, which is phase-shifted so as to be in phase with the suppressed carrier of the gonio signal. The resultant signal is fed to a superheterodyne amplitude-modulated receiver. The demodulated output of this will have a switching frequency waveform, the phase of which, in relation to the input to the balanced modulator, will now be determined. For simplicity, it will be assumed that the output of the switching oscillator is sinusoidal. The balanced modulator gives the product of the gonio signal and the switching sinusoid, i.e.

$$e_0 = A\cos\omega_s t \; [\cos\theta \cdot \cos\omega_c t] \tag{2.9}$$

where ω_c is the incoming carrier frequency, ω_s is the switching frequency, generally a low audio frequency such as 135 Hz and θ is the orientation of the goniometer rotor coil with respect to the reference direction. The term within the square brackets is the gonio output. The output e_0 is combined with the vertical antenna signal, say $B\cos\omega_c t \; (B > A)$. The input to the superheterodyne receiver is then

$$e_{in} = \cos\omega_c t \cdot A\cos\omega_s t \cdot \cos\theta + B\cos\omega_c t$$

$$= B\left[1 + \frac{A}{B}\cos\theta \cdot \cos\omega_s t\right]\cos\omega_c t \tag{2.10}$$

This expression represents a carrier of frequency ω_c amplitude modulated by a sinusoid of frequency ω_s, the phase and amplitude of the modulating signal being dependent on the value of $\cos\theta$. If $\cos\theta$ is positive $(\pi/2 > \theta > -\pi/2)$, the demodulated output is in phase and when $\cos\theta$ is negative $(\pi > \theta > \pi/2$ and $-\pi < \theta < -\pi/2)$, it is in anti-phase to the switching sinusoid $\cos\omega_s t$, as shown in Fig. 2.12. The demodulated output may be amplified and fed to

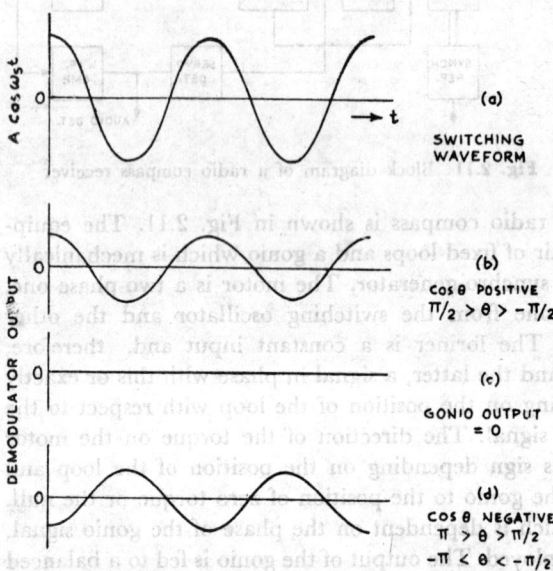

Fig. 2.12 Comparison of waveforms: (a) Switching sinusoid, and (b), (c) and (d) are Servo detector outputs for various values of θ

the second winding of the two-phase gonio motor, but an arrangement will have low power efficiency. Instead, a motor control circuit employing thyratrons is generally used. A simplified circuit of one such is shown in Fig. 2.13. The operation is as follows. The gonio motor M has two windings, one of which is supplied directly from the ac input to the transformer T_1, through a capacitor C giving a phase change of about 90°. The other winding of the

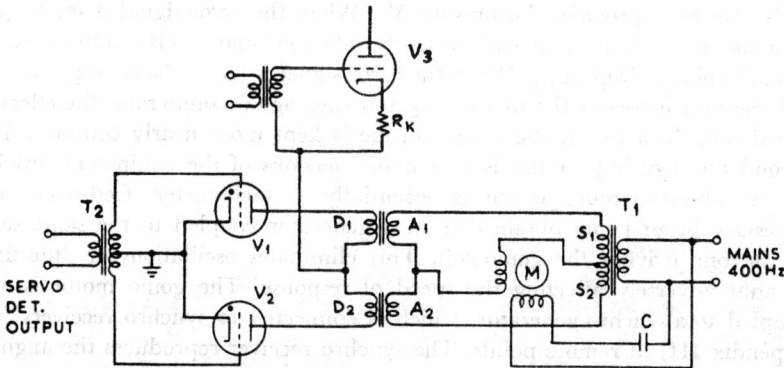

Fig. 2.13 Motor control circuit of radio compass

motor is fed from one half of the secondary of the transformer through satur-able reactors which act as switches. The saturable reactors have two windings each, the dc windings (D_1, D_2) which are connected to the thyratrons, and the ac windings (A_1, A_2) which are in the motor circuit. The impedance measured across the ac winding depends upon the current in the dc winding. If the latter is zero or very small, the impedance is high. When the current increases above a certain value, the core saturates and the impedance of the ac windings becomes very low. The saturable reactors thus act as switches which are closed when there is a current in the thyratron and open when there is no current. The phase of the voltage applied to the second winding of the motor and, therefore, the direction in which it turns, thus depends on the reactor which is saturated.

The thyratrons get their plate supply through V_3. The switching frequency sinusoid applied between the grid and cathode of V_3 is of such a magnitude that the tube conducts during the positive half cycles and is cut-off during the negative half cycles. The input to the thyratrons is obtained from the receiver and is applied to the two grids in anti-phase through the transformer T_2. The phase of the voltage at the primary depends upon the position of the gonio-coil and will be in phase or 180° out of phase with the reference signal and of course will be zero at the nulls. If it is in phase, one of the thyratrons (say V_1) will conduct and if it is in anti-phase, the other (V_2) will conduct. The direction in which the motor turns depends upon the position of the gonio-coil and it can be shown that the coil attains the equilibrium position in one of the nulls. The demonstration of this is left to the student.

The gonio, the receiver and the motor constitute a feed-back control system and the details of its behaviour such as its tendency to hunt about its equi-librium position and the closeness with which it follows a changing null may be studied by application of feed-back theory. These aspects will not be dealt with here. Mention is, however, made of two points relevant to this. The first is the use of the resistor R_k in the cathode of V_3 as shown in Fig. 2.13.

This resistance provides the bias for V_3. When the error signal is small, (i.e. near the null), the average current tends to be low, and this is counteracted by a small voltage drop in R_k. When the error signal is large, the average current is large and increases the bias on V_3 and thus again counteracts the effect of the signal. As a result, the motor torque is kept more nearly constant. The second point of importance is that many versions of the equipment provide an 'anti-hunt' circuit, which is essentially a tachometer feed-back, the necessary input being obtained from a generator coupled to the same shaft as the one driving the gonio-coil. This eliminates oscillations or 'hunting' without adversely affecting the speed of response. The gonio motor is also coupled to a synchro generator, which is connected to synchro receivers (see appendix III) at remote points. The synchro receiver reproduces the angular position of the generator (and, therefore, of the loop), and thus performs the fi nction of a bearing indicator.

The radio compass is one of the most widely used navigational aids. Though it does not give very precise bearings, its simplicity and the large number of ground transmitting stations available for obtaining bearings have made it a common item of aircraft navigational equipment. Modern versions of the installation employ ferrite cored loops and transistorized electronic equipment. The antennas are made very flat and can be so mounted on the fuselage, so that the drag is very low, facilitating their use on high speed aircraft. Some receivers are provided with crystal tuning for increased stability.

(b) A VHF Phase-comparison Automatic Direction-Finder

The principle of operation of this DF can be understood if one examines the nature of the output obtained from an Adcock aerial to which the output of a vertical aerial situated in the centre is added. As an Adcock pair is equivalent to a loop aerial, the output may be expressed in the form given below.

$$e_0 = (K + \cos\theta)\cos\omega t \qquad (2.6)$$

where K is the ratio of the peak amplitudes of the vertical and Adcock antennas and θ the angle which the plane of the aerial makes with the direction of arrival of the signal. For convenience, let the angles be measured from North and let ϕ be the direction of arrival and ψ the angle which the plane of the antenna makes with the North. Then in Eq. 2.6

$$\theta = \psi - \phi$$

Let the antenna be rotated with an angular velocity ω_s, so that

$$\psi = \omega_s t \text{ and}$$
$$e_0 = [K + \cos(\omega_s t - \phi)]\cos\omega t \qquad (2.11)$$

This is an amplitude modulated signal. When it is demodulated in an envelope detector, the variable component of the output obtained is proportional to $\cos(\omega_s t - \phi)$.

Suppose a reference sinusoid of the same frequency (ω_s) is obtained by coupling an alternator to the rotating antenna. By suitably positioning the poles of the alternator, one can obtain from it the sinusoid $\cos\omega_s t$. The phase difference between the demodulated receiver output and the alternator

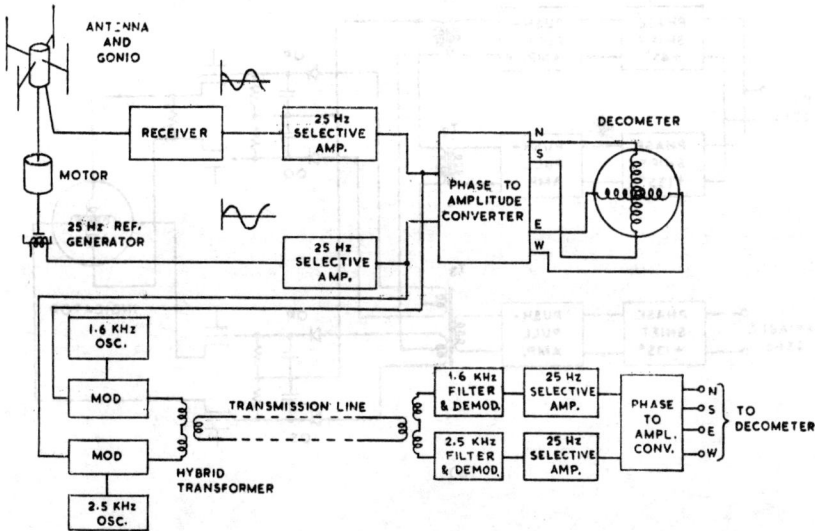

Fig. 2.14 Block diagram of VHF automatic direction-finder (Marconi ADF)

voltage, i.e. the angle ϕ, gives the direction of arrival of the signal. The bearing may, therefore, be read off directly on a phase measuring device. This is the basic principle of some VHF DFs employing the phase-comparison technique. A block diagram of one such equipment[8] is shown in Fig. 2.14 and its operation is explained in what follows.

The DF employs a pair of fixed Adcock antennas with a capacitance goniometer to obtain the rotating figure-of-eight pattern. Instead of using a vertical antenna for obtaining a fixed phase signal, an unbalanced output is taken from the capacitance goniometer rotor. The vector sum of the voltages induced in the rotor, when combined with the figure-of-eight pattern gives the required cardioid as represented in Eq. 2.6. The gonio rotor is coupled to a motor and rotated at 25 rps. To the same shaft is attached an ac generator which gives a 25 Hz ac voltage of fixed reference phase. The signal from the goniometer, which is modulated at 25 Hz by the rotation of the rotor, is applied to the receiver and after demodulation and amplification is passed through a selective amplifier and is applied to a phase measuring device along with the signal from the reference generator. For remote indication, the two 25 Hz signals are made to amplitude modulate two audio frequency carriers which are then transmitted to the remote point where they are demodulated and the two modulating 25 Hz signals are recovered. These are then applied to a phase-meter.

The phase-meter and the associated circuits are shown in Fig. 2.15(a). The meter is provided with two coils whose axes are at right angles to each other and in the centre is a small permanent magnet mounted on a spindle to which the indicating pointer is attached. When two direct currents are passed in the coils, the magnet aligns itself with the resultant magnetic field.

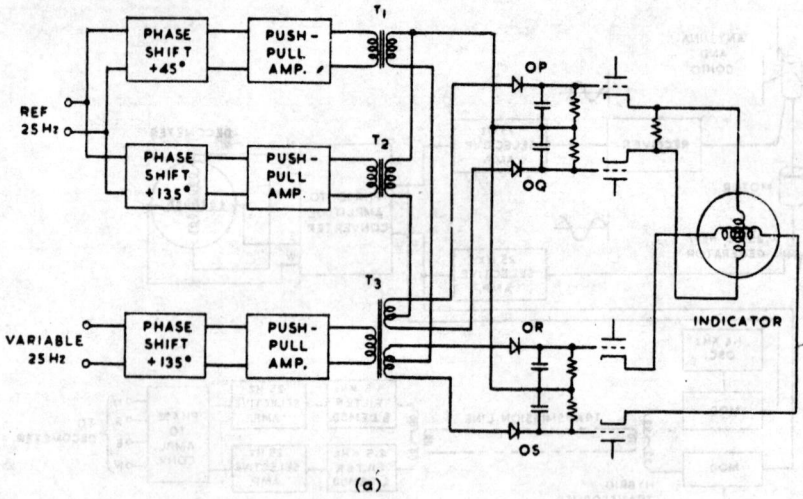

(a)

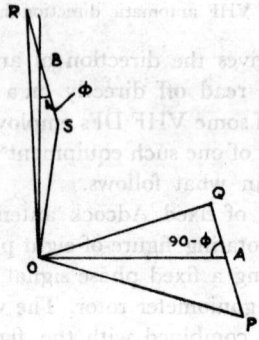

(b)

Fig. 2.15 (a) Circuit of the phase measuring part of the receiver and (b) phasor diagram of voltages in the circuit

The angle to which it turns is such that the tangent of this angle is equal to the ratio of the currents in the two coils. If these two currents are made proportional to cos ϕ and sin ϕ, the position of the pointer will directly indicate the direction of arrival of the electromagnetic wave. The circuit shown in Fig. 2.15(a) is the phase-to-amplitude discriminator which performs the function of giving output currents proportional to cosϕ and sinϕ when provided with two inputs cos $\omega_s t$ and cos $(\omega_s t - \phi)$. Its operation is as follows. The reference signal is split into two components by phase-splitting networks and amplified by push-pull amplifiers to obtain two equal voltages in phase quadrature in the secondaries of the transformers T_1 and T_2. These are represented by phasors OA and OB [Fig. 2.15(b)], which lead the original reference voltage in the primary by 45° and 135° respectively. The variable phase signal is applied to a similar phase-splitting network and amplified and two equal outputs are obtained from two centre-tapped secondaries of transformer T_3. These outputs lead the variable phase input by 135°. The secondaries of the transformers are connected in such a manner as to add the voltages in each half of the secondaries of T_3 to the quadrature reference voltages, giving the four phasor quantities.

$$\overrightarrow{OP} = \overrightarrow{OA} + \overrightarrow{AP}; \quad \overrightarrow{OQ} = \overrightarrow{OA} + \overrightarrow{AQ}$$
$$\overrightarrow{OR} = \overrightarrow{OB} + \overrightarrow{BR}; \quad \overrightarrow{OS} = \overrightarrow{OB} + \overrightarrow{BS}$$

The variable phase signal is much smaller than the reference phase voltage. The above relations may then be approximated as follows

$$OP = OA + AP \cos(90 - \phi) = OA + AP \sin\phi$$
$$OQ = OA - AP \sin\phi$$
$$OR = OB + BR \cos\phi, \quad OS = OB - BR \cos\phi$$

The voltages are rectified and the resultant direct voltages, which are nearly equal to the peak ac input are applied to the grids of the tubes V_1, V_2, V_3 and V_4. The currents which flow in the windings of the phase-meter are proportional to the difference between the corresponding grid voltages at the tubes. The differences are equal to 2AP $\sin\phi$ and 2 BR $\cos\phi$, but as AP and BR are equal (as the secondaries of T_3 are identical), they are proportional to the sine and cosine of the phase angle ϕ, which is also the bearing angle.

To maintain the desired accuracy in this type of instrument, the various components must be accurately constructed and must maintain stable values. Some octantal error arises in the instrument as the variable phase signal is not very small compared with the reference phase one, but this is made to cancel the octantal error arising in the capacitance goniometer. The overall accuracy may be as high as about 1°.

The DF operates on a VHF radio telephony channel. The speech frequencies are modulated at 25 Hz by the goniometer and intelligibility is impaired. To overcome this drawback, the receiver output going to the speech channels is demodulated by applying a 25 Hz voltage to variable gain amplifiers.

2.9 The Commutated Aerial Direction-Finder

We have so far considered DFs which employ antenna of dimensions small compared with the wavelength. If the width of the antenna (b in Eq. 1.1) is increased beyond several wavelengths, the antenna will have a multiple lobe polar diagram and cannot be used in the same manner as the smaller one for direction finding. Such an antenna, called a wide-aperture antenna would, however, have the advantage of reduced site errors. Site errors arise because objects in the site tend to produce local distortions in the wavefront. A small aperture antenna is affected by these but a large aperture antenna, of a width of many wavelengths, tends to even out the effect of these distortions and reduce site errors. But different techniques (rather than null location) have to be used to utilize the wide aperture antenna. The 'commutated aerial direction-finder' (CADF) employs the method described in what follows.

Consider an antenna system consisting of two antennas A and B (Fig. 2.16) separated by a distance of less than $\frac{\lambda}{2}$ and rotated around the circumference of a circle of radius $r(r \gg \lambda)$.

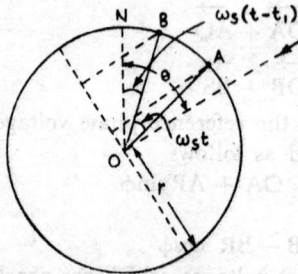

Fig. 2.16
Rotation of two antennas a circle inproducing phase modulation

Let ω_s be the angular velocity of rotation of the antennas about the centre 0 and $\omega_s t_1$, the angle subtended by the two antennas at 0. Consider an electromagnetic wave incident from a direction making an angle θ with the North. The phases of the voltage in the two antennas, (with respect to a reference phase at 0) are then:

$$\phi_1 = \frac{2\pi r}{\lambda} \cos (\omega_s t - \theta) \text{ in } B$$

$$\phi_2 = \frac{2\pi r}{\lambda} \cos (\omega_s t - t_1 - \theta) \text{ in } A \qquad 2.12$$

The phase difference ϕ between these two voltages is thus

$$\phi = \phi_1 - \phi_2 = \frac{2\pi r}{\lambda} \left[\cos (\omega_s t - \theta) - \cos (\omega_s t - t_1 - \theta) \right]$$

$$= \frac{2\pi r}{\lambda} \cdot 2\sin \frac{\omega_s t_1}{2} \cdot \sin \left(\omega_s t - \theta - \frac{\omega_s t_1}{2} \right)$$

Since the chord length AB $= 2r \cdot \sin \left(\frac{\omega_s t_1}{2} \right)$,

$$\phi = \frac{2\pi}{\lambda} \text{ AB} \cos (\omega_s t - t_1/2 - \theta) \qquad 2.13$$

If the signals from A and B are applied to a phase detector, the output voltage will be proportional to $\cos (\omega_s t - \theta - \omega_s t_1/2)$. The bearing θ may be obtained by phase comparison with a reference signal $\cos \omega_s t$, which can be obtained from the antenna rotation. This is the basic method employed for determining θ. In practical implementation, instead of rotating the antenna-pair, a number of antennas are fixed at equal distances along the circumference of a circle and the signals from pairs of these antennas are seqeuentially sampled. For details of the implementation, see Ref. 9,10. The term 'commutated aerial direction-finder' arises because of this technique.

The CADF gives improved performance over the Adcock system, not only in the presence of site imperfections but also when multipath transmissions and interfering signals are present.

2.10 Range and Accuracy of Direction-Finders

Ground-based direction-finders are generally of the Adcock type and are relatively free from polarization errors. In day time, such installations when installed on a good site have the limiting accuracy of the instrumentation, generally of the goniometer, which may be under 1°, if calibrated. At night time, when sky-wave propagation is predominant, errors will arise which may range from 2° to 4° depending on the distance of the transmitter (150 to 600 km)*. Most ground-based Adcock stations operate between 2 and 3 MHz and serve ships. Such stations are not suitable for aircraft as aircraft transmissions are generally confined to much higher frequencies because of the difficulties associated with equipping the aircraft with efficient antennas operating in this range.

Ground-based VHF DFs are widely used, particularly in civil aviation. Their range is mainly limited by the line-of-sight propagation. The principal errors are due to the site. When such direction-finders are installed in an airport, these errors can be quite large. But with the provision of remote indication (as in ADF), the DF can be installed in a good site and the errors reduced. The commutated antenna DF enables a further reduction of site errors by a large factor.

Airborne DFs are generally of the loop type and operate in the MF/LF band. Reliable operation is possible with ground waves up to several hundred miles under favourable conditions. Accuracies up to 2° (after correcting for aircraft quadrantal errors) are possible. At night times, sky waves contaminate the signal and long range operation is not possible. Under these conditions, fairly reliable operation is possible only at the lower end of the frequency range and up to much shorter distances (less than 150 km). The calibration of these DFs holds only at one frequency and the condition of pitch and roll may also alter it. Taking all these factors into consideration, the bearings obtained from ground wave cannot be relied on to better than $\pm 5°$.

In spite of the errors in the bearing determined, the aircraft (or ship) can always use the bearing for 'homing', i.e. going towards the transmitter. In the case of aircraft, when flying over the transmitter, a rapid reversal of bearing takes place. This gives an indication of the position of the aircraft. I: the case of ships, it is inadvisable to home on to a beacon, because of the risk of collision. Transmitters transmitting continuous waves or modulated continuous waves are widely used in civil aviation for navigational assistance. These are called 'non-directional beacons'.

---

* In literature on Navigation, distances are often given in Nautical Miles and Statute Miles and speed in Knots. The following conversion factors may then be used.

1 Nautical Mile	= 1·85 kM
1 Statute Mile	= 1·61 kM
1 Knot	= 1·85 kM/hr

3
Radio Ranges

RADIO ranges are navigational aids which are mainly used by aircraft. There are two types of radio ranges in use, the low frequency four-course radio range and the VHF omni-directional radio range. The former can be used by any aircraft equipped with a receiver which can tune to the frequency of the ground station, which is in the LF/MF range of 200-400 kHz, while the latter requires special equipment. The LF/MF radio range is obsolescent and so only a brief treatment of the principles of its operation is given. The VHF omni-range (generally abbreviated as VOR) is in use in most parts of the world.

3.1 The LF/MF Four-course Radio Range

The LF/MF radio range employs two antenna systems each of which has a polar diagram of the figure-of-eight type, these two being at right angles to each other [Fig. 3.1(a)]. The points of intersection of these two figures-of-eight, when joined to the centre, give four directions in which the signals from

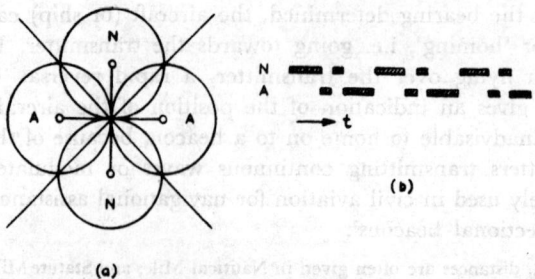

Fig. 3.1 (a) Polar diagram of the four-course radio range and (b) interlacing A and N transmissions

the two sets of antennas have the same strength. These are called equi-signal courses. A transmitter is made to energize these antennas alternately by a relay called the link circuit relay. In order to distinguish the transmission from the two antennas, one of them is made to transmit the letter N (— .) in morse and the other to transmit the letter A (. —) the two being inter-locked as shown in Fig. 3.1(b). Both these transmissions are modulated by an audio frequency note of 1020 Hz. When the aircraft is on course, the two signals being equal, a continuous note of 1020 Hz is heard. At points off the course, either the letter N or the letter A is predominant. Owing to the fact that the ear can distinguish only a finite change in the intensity of the signal, the equi-signal course appears spread over a small angle, generally about 3°. The radio range, thus provides four paths at right angles along which the aircraft can navigate. These paths are arranged to be along the most useful routes.

In a variation of this system, called the SRA (Simultaneous Range Adcock) five antenna towers are used, four at the corners of a square and the fifth at the centre. Power is fed to all the antennas. The transmissions from the corner towers give rise to two figure-of-eight polar diagrams. The transmissions from the centre tower, which differs in frequency by 1020 Hz, combines with the others to give four equi-signal courses. In addition, by a combination of the power and phase of radio frequency energy fed to the four corner antennas, the figure-of-eight patterns can be reduced or increased in size and the two lobes of the pattern can be made unequal. This enables one to obtain courses which are not perpendicular to each other, as shown in Fig. 3.2. These are

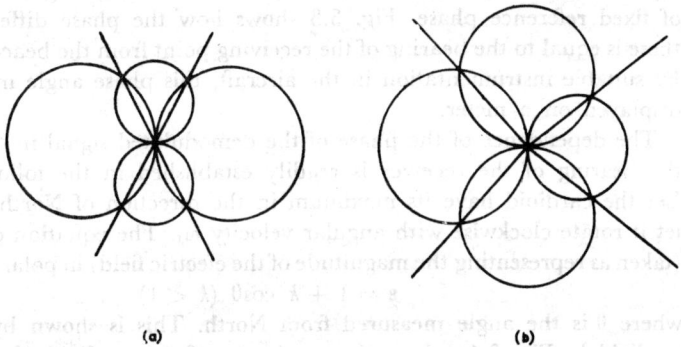

                    (a)   (b)

Fig. 3.2 (a) Course-shifting and (b) course-bending in LF/MF radio range

called course-bending and course-shifting. In addition, by feeding the power to the antennas through a goniometer, rotation of the courses is also made possible. In this system, it is possible to arrange the courses to serve routes which are not necessarily perpendicular to each other. The radiation from the central antenna can also be modulated to serve as radio telephony channel to broadcast weather news.

The radio range facility gives good service over a range of about 200 Km. The transmission from the central tower can be used for radio compass operation also. The disadvantages of the range are (1) the limited number of courses (i.e. four) available, (2) poor signal/noise ratio, (3) fatigue caused by listening to the tones, and (4) difficulty of identifying the course. These factors, and the emergence of the VHF omni-range have contributed to the obsolescence of the LF/MF radio range.

3.2   VHF Omni-directional Range (VOR)

This facility operates in the range 108—136 MHz in the VHF band. An aircraft provided with the appropriate receiving equipment can obtain its radial position with respect to the range by comparing the phases of two sinusoids obtained from the range radiation. Any fixed phase difference defines a radial course and so, in effect, the VOR may be regarded as providing an infinite number of courses, as against the four of the LF/MF radio range. The principle of operation is given in what follows.

The range transmitter radiates two patterns, distinguishable by different modulations, one of which is omni-directional and carries the modulation of a reference 30 Hz sinusoid, while the second pattern is a figure-of-eight rotating at 30 rps. The radio frequency phases of the two are locked. The omni-directional radiation has a much stronger field than the figure-of-eight one, and, therefore, the combination gives rise to a rotating cardioid. At the receiving point, the rotating cardioid, after demodulation, gives a 30 Hz signal of variable phase, while the omni-directional signal gives a 30 Hz signal of fixed reference phase. Fig. 3.3 shows how the phase difference between these is equal to the bearing of the receiving point from the beacon transmitter. By suitable instrumentation in the aircraft, this phase angle may be directly displayed on a meter.

The dependence of the phase of the demodulated signal in the receiver on the bearing of the receiver is readily established in the following manner. Let the cardioid have its maximum in the direction of North at $t = 0$ and let it rotate clockwise with angular velocity ω_s. The equation of the cardioid (taken as representing the magnitude of the electric field) in polar coordinates is:

$$\varepsilon = 1 + k \, \cos\theta \; (k < 1) \tag{3.1}$$

where θ is the angle measured from North. This is shown by the full line cardioid in Fig. 3.4, where the maximum of the cardioid ($\theta = 0$) is in the direction of North. At a time t, when the cardioid has turned by angle $\omega_s t$, the field magnitude in a direction ϕ is given by the same equation but with θ replaced by $\phi - \omega_s t$, as is clear from the cardioid shown by the broken line in Fig. 3.4. The signal received by a receiver in the direction θ is, therefore, proportional to $1 + k \, \cos(\phi - \omega_s t)$, which has a sinusoidal component of angular frequency ω_s. By comparing the phase difference between this and a signal $\cos \omega_s t$, the angle ϕ, which is the desired bearing, can be determined.

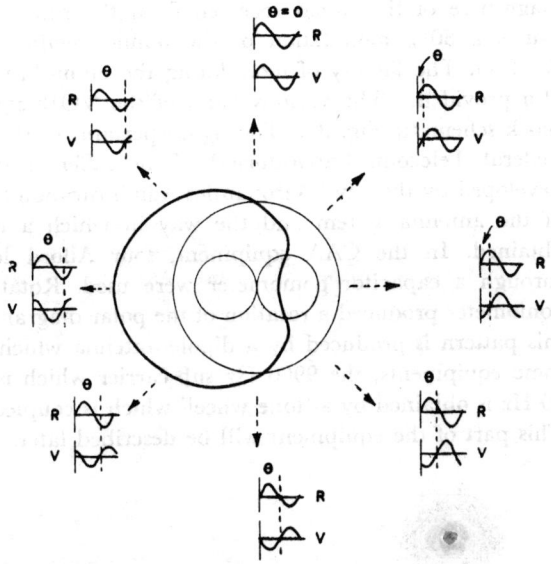

Fig. 3.3 Reference (**R**) and variable-phase (**V**) signals of VOR received at various points

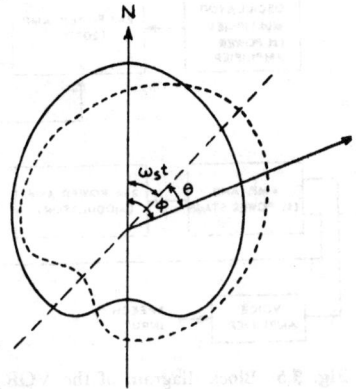

Fig. 3.4
Production of variable phase signal by rotation of the cardioid pattern

Note that the reference signal and the variable phase signal are in phase when the receiver is due North of the beacon.

As the omni-directional and figure-of-eight patterns have the same carrier frequency, the reference sinusoid cannot be made to directly amplitude modulate the former. To enable separation, the following method is employed. The radio frequency power fed to the omni-directional antenna is amplitude modulated to a depth of 30% by a subcarrier with a mean frequency of 9960 Hz which is itself frequency modulated at 30 Hz, the maximum frequency deviation being 480 Hz. The variable phase signal is produced, as stated earlier, by the rotation of the phase locked figure-of-eight pattern. The magnitude of the signal received from the rotating pattern is such that it causes a 30% modulation of the omni-directional carrier (i.e. $k = 0.3$ in Eq. 3.1). The facility of modulating the omni-directional pattern by voice is also provided. The various parts of the VOR equipment are shown in the block schematic Fig. 3.5. The figure pertains to the equipment developed by Federal Telecom. Laboratories[11]. This differs from the earlier equipment developed by the Civil Aeronautics Administration (CAA)[12], mainly in respect of the antenna system and the way in which a rotating figure-of-eight is obtained. In the CAA equipment, four Alford loop antennas, energized through a capacitor goniometer were used. Rotation of the stator of the goniometer produced a rotation of the polar diagram. In the FTL equipment, this pattern is produced by a dipole antenna which is itself rotated. In both these equipments, the 9960 Hz sub-carrier which is frequency modulated at 30 Hz is obtained by a 'tone wheel' which is coupled to the rotating element. This part of the equipment will be described later.

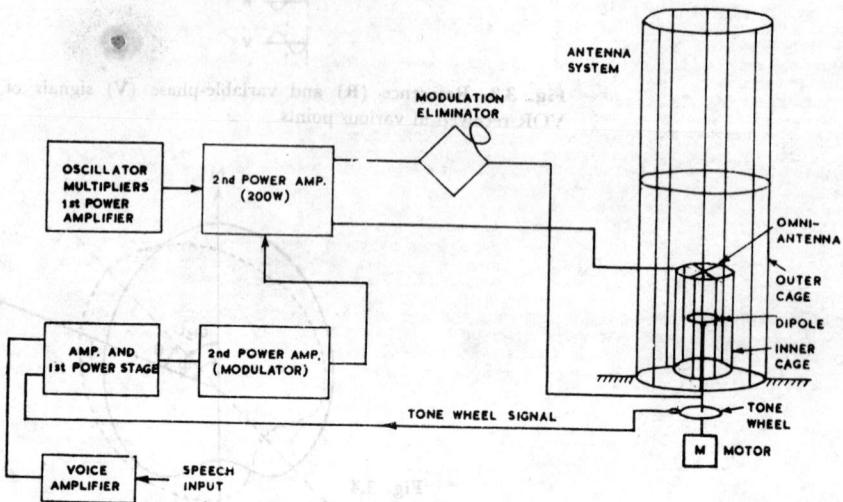

Fig. 3.5 Block diagram of the VOR ground equipment

Referring to Fig. 3.5, the transmitter consists of a crystal controlled oscillator, frequency multipliers and a driver, and a power amplifier. The power amplifier is amplitude modulated by the modulator which is given an input consisting of the tone wheel signal (9960 Hz sub-carrier) and when desired, a voice signal. The output of the power amplifier is divided into two parts, the greater part (about 90%) of which goes directly to the omni-directional antenna. The remaining part is passed through a modulation eliminator and energizes the rotating antenna. (In the CAA equipment, it goes to the rotor of the goniometer.)

The antenna system is a special cage-type one developed for this purpose and a detailed description of it is given in Ref. 11 and 13. It consists of a disc-type antenna with four slots which gives the omni-directional pattern and a rotating dipole which produces the figure-of-eight pattern. The latter is enclosed in a double-cage made up of vertical rods and two end-plates which act as a radial waveguide coupled to free-space through vertical slots. The dipole is only a tenth of a wavelength long but because of its position within the waveguide, it presents a resistive impedance. The outer of the two cages enclosing the antennas is extended up by 12 feet. The net result of the antenna structure is to give a radiation made up of the two required patterns, the polarization of the radiation being horizontal. This antenna is also simple to adjust for correct operation, as the difficulty of properly phasing the four Alford loops in the older type of equipment is eliminated by the use of a rotating antenna.

The 30 Hz reference phase signal, as stated earlier, is transmitted in the form of a frequency modulation of a 9960 Hz sub-carrier. This modulated carrier is obtained from the tone wheel attached to the motor which rotates the dipole aerial. Thus, in effect, the two 30 Hz signals are generated by the rotations of the same motor and, therefore, have exactly the same frequency. A part of the tone wheel is shown in detail in Fig. 3.6. The tone wheel is like

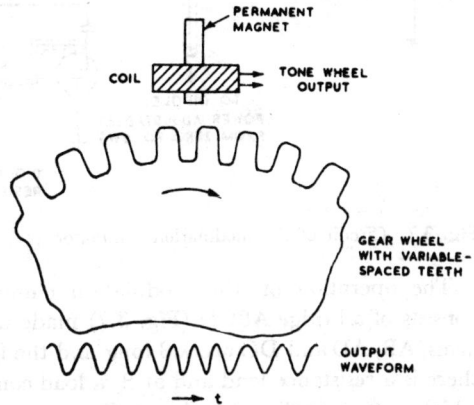

Fig. 3.6
Detail of the tone wheel

a gear wheel, made of magnetic material. A permanent magnet with a coil around it is placed close to the periphery of the wheel. Rotation of the wheel induces a voltage in this coil. The teeth of the wheel are non-uniformly spaced to give a sinusoidally frequency-modulated output. The tone wheel output, which is about 0·6 mW in a 600 ohm load, is amplified and made to amplitude modulate the transmitter. The relative positions of the tone wheel and the dipole antenna are made adjustable to enable the alignment of the 0° phase difference course with the true North.

The importance of maintaining the phase relation between the carrier of the omni-directional radiation and of the figure-of-eight radiation has already been mentioned. This requirement is met by first modulating the carrier, then separating a part of it and removing its modulation. If, on the other hand, two separate power amplifiers were used for the modulated and unmodulated outputs, there is a possibility that the phase angle between the two carriers will change due to small changes of tuning. This method is, therefore, not employed and instead a modulation eliminator, the circuit of which is shown in Fig. 3.7, is employed.

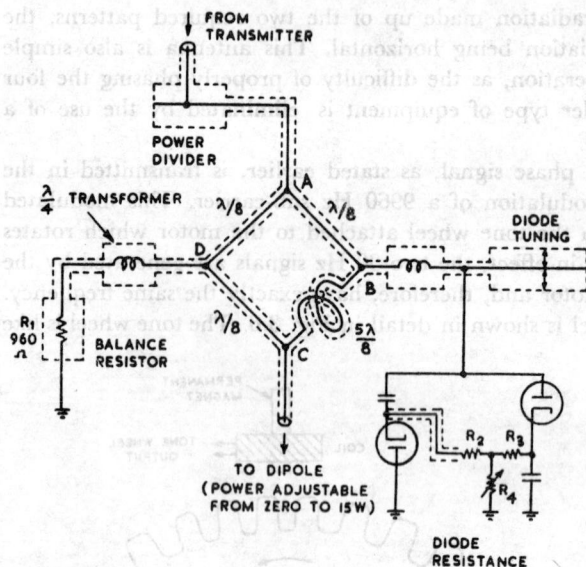

Fig. 3.7 Circuit of the modulation-eliminator

The operation of the modulation eliminator is as follows. The circuit consists of a bridge ABCD (Fig. 3.7) made up of coaxial lines, in which three arms, AB, AD and DC are $\lambda/8$ long and the fourth arm BC is $5/8\lambda$ long. At D, there is a resistance load and at B, a load consisting of two special VHF diodes which act as nonlinear resistors. The power arriving from A to C takes two paths, one via D and the other via B, and as these two are in anti-phase (because the arm BC is $\lambda/2$ longer than the others), the resultant voltage is the difference between the two. If the bridge is balanced, (i.e. if the impedances presented at D and B are equal), there will be no net output. The power arriving by the path ADC may be taken to be a constant fraction of the input power, as there is a linear resistance termination at D. The power arriving via ABC, however, depends upon the value of the terminating resistance presented by the diode circuit, which depends upon the actual voltage applied. The special diodes used have a characteristic such that for inputs below a certain value, they can be approximated by a linear resistance while for high inputs, saturation occurs and the slope resistance becomes high.

The value of the load resistance due to the balance resistor appearing at the point D is high (about $7\frac{1}{2}$ times the characteristic impedance of the transmission line) and, therefore, little power flows into it. Most of the power is transmitted to C. In the other path ABC, below the saturation voltage, the diode circuit presents a very low impedance and only a small fraction of the input voltage appears at C. There is thus a net voltage at C which is the difference between the larger voltage coming via ADC and the smaller voltage coming via ABC. Above the saturation voltage, the diodes act as high resistances and the impedance presented at B is made equal to that at D. The bridge is, therefore, balanced and the excess voltage above the critical value gets cancelled out at C. The critical voltage is set to a value which corresponds to the modulation trough. The output at C then will be proportional to the input up to an amplitude corresponding to the modulation trough and beyond that it remains constant. The modulation is thus eliminated.

In a practical modulation eliminator, the bridge may consist of coaxial lines of 50 ohm characteristic impedance. The linear resistance at D has a value of about 400 ohms. On the other side, the diodes present a forward resistance of about 80 ohms when not saturated, which is transformed to 16 ohms at the point B by a quarter-wave transformer. Most of the power is, therefore, absorbed here and very little goes to the point C. When the diodes are saturated they present a high resistance. They also come in series with the resistors R_2, R_3 and R_4 which combine to present the resistance required at B to balance the bridge. The resistor R_4 is made adjustable to achieve exact balance. The modulation eliminator has an efficiency of about 23% and delivers about 15 W to the rotating antenna.

3.3 VOR Receiving Equipment

The air-borne equipment which can utilize the VOR facility consists of a broad band omni-directional antenna, a multichannel amplitude modulated receiver which can be tuned over the required band, and an instrumentation unit which processes the receiver output to obtain the course indication. In most of the modern installations, a common receiver is used for the reception of VOR and ILS signals (see Chapter 6) and the demodulated output is switched to the required instrumentation and display circuits. The frequency band over which the receiver works is 108·0 to 135·95 mHz covering 560 allocations each separated from the adjacent ones by 50 kHz. Continuous tuning over this range is not desirable. Modern receivers are crystal controlled and tuned to spot frequencies. By a system of multiple heterodyning, the 560 channels are obtained with a limited number of crystals, as explained in Appendix II. Transistorized circuits are used in some receivers.

The essential elements of the instrumentation part of the receiver are shown in the block diagram of Fig. 3.8. The demodulated output of the receiver, which is the input to the instrumentation unit contains the variable phase 30 Hz signal and the reference phase signal as frequency

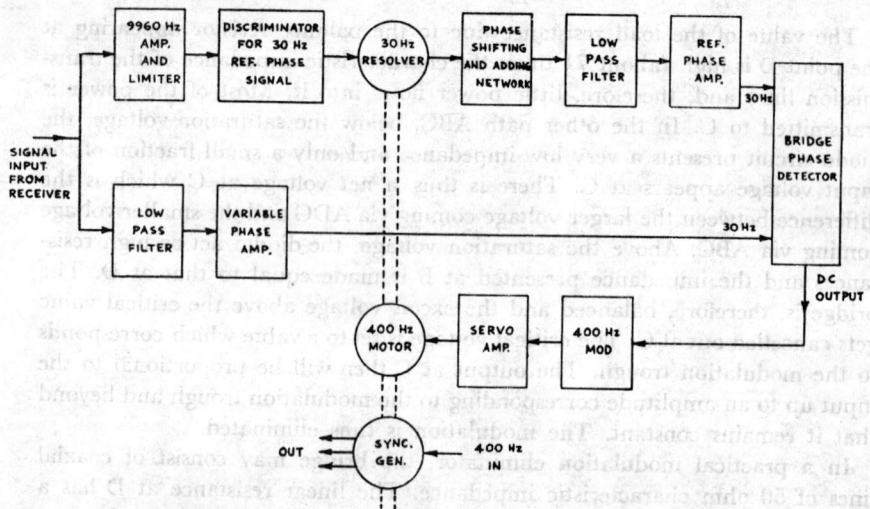

Fig. 3.8 Instrumentation part of VOR receiver

modulation on the 9960 Hz sub-carrier. These are separated by filters into two channels. The reference phase signal is passed through an amplitude limiter, a discriminator and a low pass amplifier to obtain the 30 Hz modulation. The variable phase signal is similarly amplified by a low pass amplifier. (It must be ensured that the phase changes introduced in these two branches are equal, as otherwise, the course will be in error by the difference between the two phase shifts.) The two 30 Hz signals thus become available and the phase difference between them is to be displayed. This is done by a feed-back arrangement utilizing a resolver, a phase-detector and a motor, as shown in Fig. 3.8. The resolver is a sine-cosine generator used to produce an angular phase-shift that is precisely equivalent to the angular position of its shaft (*see* Appendix-III). The reference phase signal is given to the resolver and its output is filtered, amplified and applied to the phase detector. The variable phase signal is also applied to the phase detector. The output of this circuit is a dc voltage, the magnitude and polarity of which depends on the phase difference between the two inputs. The dc output goes to a balanced modulator which has a 400 Hz ac switching input, and its output is a 400 Hz voltage, the magnitude and phase of which depend upon the magnitude and polarity of the dc input. The ac output is applied, after amplification, to a motor which is coupled to the resolver. The feed-back loop is thus completed and the motor turns the resolver until the phase detector output is zero, i.e. until the phase change brought about by the resolver is equal to the phase difference between the reference and variable phase signals. The shaft position of the resolver then indicates the phase difference between the reference and variable phase signals, i.e. the direction of the craft with respect to the omni-range. The position of the shaft may be conveyed to any location in the aircraft (e.g. the pilot's control panel) by a synchro system.

3.4 Range and Accuracy of VOR

As the operating frequency is in the VHF band, the range of the VOR facility is essentially the line-of-sight range, extended approximately 10-15% by refraction effects. The line-of-sight range depends upon the height of the VOR antenna and of the aircraft. The useable range is in addition limited by signal/noise considerations and for very high flying aircraft is limited to about 400-500 km. For an aircraft flying at 6000 m (20,000 ft), the range is about 335 km.

The overall error of the VOR system is made up of errors arising from the following sources:

    (a)   ground station and aircraft equipment,

    (b)   site irregularities,

    (c)   terrain features, and

    (d)   polarization.

(a)   The ground station equipment error is mainly the octantal error in the installations using two antenna pairs and a rotating goniometer for obtaining the rotating figure-of-eight pattern. Octantal error can also arise owing to inhomogeneity in the ground characteristics at the installation and could, therefore, occur even where rotating antennas are used. Equipment error in the receiver and indicator in the aircraft arise owing to imperfections of the circuits and components such as those contained in the feed-back control system. The magnitudes of the equipment errors are best specified in terms of the probability distribution. Analysis of a large number of ground station errors indicates[14] that the error distribution is Gaussian, with a 95% probability that the error is within 2°.

(b)   Site errors arise when the signal arrives at the receiver by two paths, one directly from the range and the other after reflection from objects in the neighbourhood of the range. The reference phase signal is not appreciably affected by this, as the difference in the path delays is always small compared with the period of the modulation cycle. The variable phase components may, however, differ appreciably. Referring to Fig. 3.9, the signal arriving directly

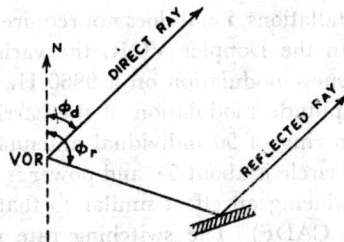

Fig. 3.9
Error due to site irregularity

at the receiver has the variable phase component with a phase difference ϕ_d with respect to the reference signal while the reflected signal has a phase difference ϕ_r. The carriers of the two signals are also not in phase generally.

The combination of the two variable phase signals produces, after demodulation, a 30 Hz signal, the phase of which is different from both ϕ_d and ϕ_r. The analysis of the error is given in Ref. 13. The magnitude of the error depends upon the relative strengths of the direct and reflected signals as well as upon ϕ_d and ϕ_r. Because of this last quantity, the error varies as the aircraft moves along a radial line, keeping ϕ_d constant resulting in slow bends in the course. Site errors cannot easily be eliminated and, therefore, considerable effort has been devoted to improving the performance of the VOR by refinements of technique. One such development is mentioned in the next section.

(c)   Terrain errors are those appearing even at considerable distance from the VOR station, owing to the nature of the terrain (e.g. hills, lakes, mountain ranges, etc.) which changes the path of propagation. These errors occur in the immediate vicinity of the interfering objects and appear as rapid fluctuations ('Scalloping') in the course-deviation indicator.

(d)   Polarization error arises because of the vertical component of the radiated electric field, which has a polar diagram different from that of the horizontal component. The error can be reduced by minimizing the vertically polarized component radiated by the ground antenna and by making the aircraft antenna insensitive to vertically polarized signals. The latter alone cannot provide a complete solution, because the aircraft has to bank in the course of maneuvers and, however, good the antenna, it will then inevitably respond to the vertical field. Suppression of the vertical component from the transmitted radiation is, therefore important, particularly for radiation at higher angles.

3.5   Recent Developments

Though VOR is widely used, its performance falls short of the most stringent requirements demanded of navigational aids. The principal deficiency is its proneness to site errors, and their elimination has attracted considerable developmental effort. The Doppler VOR system has been developed by CAA in the United States and is claimed to give a reduction of site errors by a factor of 7 and has the merit that it is completely compatible with existing installations, i.e. it does not require any modification of the aircraft equipment.

In the Doppler VOR, the variable phase signal is transmitted as the frequency modulation on a 9960 Hz sub-carrier and the reference phase as the amplitude modulation of the carrier at 30 Hz. The antenna system consists of a ring of 50 individual antennas and a central antenna. The diameter of the circle is about 5λ and power is switched consecutively to the 50 antennas, producing an effect similar to that of the rotation of a single antenna (as in the CADF). The switching rate is such as to produce 30 revolutions per second. At the receiver, the effective rotation of the antenna produces a frequency modulation with a maximum frequency deviation of 480 Hz. The carrier radiated by the outer aerials is made 9960 Hz higher than that from the central aerial. Therefore, the resultant field appears to have an amplitude modulation at 9960 Hz which is frequency modulated at 30 Hz with a frequency deviation of 480 Hz. The phase of the modulation clearly depends upon the bearing of the receiver, as the frequency deviation is maximum when the antenna is moving in the direction of the receiver (either towards or away from it), and is zero when it is moving at right angles to this direction.

Field studies of Doppler VOR have shown that site errors and bends under comparable site conditions are reduced by a factor of four to seven. The disadvantage of the Doppler VOR is the greater complexity of the ground equipment and the large area required for the installation. (A 50 m diameter counterpoise was used in the developmental models).

The site errors having been reduced by the wide aperture antenna employed in Doppler VOR the remaining errors are principally instrumental ones. In a developmental system, these errors are sought to be reduced by the use of a multilobe technique similar to that in TACAN (see Chapter 5). This system requires[15] changes in the receiver equipment and has so far not been widely adopted.

4

Hyperbolic Systems of Navigation

Loran and Decca

HYPERBOLIC systems are based on the measurement of the difference in the time of arrival of electromagnetic waves from two transmitters to the receiver in the craft. The name arises from the fact that the locus of points which have a constant value of such a delay is a hyperbola on a plane surface. Currently, two systems which use this principle are in use, namely Loran and Decca.

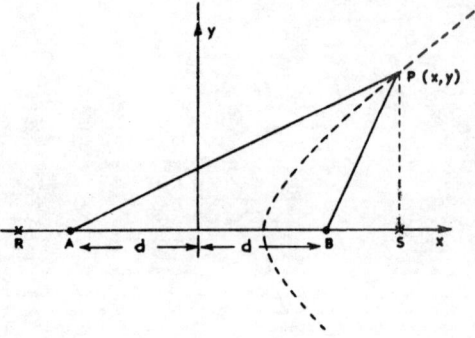

Fig. 4.1
Analysis of a hyperbolic system (A and B are transmitters and P is the receiver)

Referring to Fig. 4.1, let us assume that station A and station B make synchronous transmissions and that some means is provided in the receiver at P to measure the interval between the times of arrival of the radiations from the two stations. This interval $t_d = \dfrac{AP}{c} - \dfrac{BP}{c}$, where c is the velocity of electromagnetic waves. Taking the coordinates of P as (x, y) with reference to the axes shown in the figure, we have

$$AP = \sqrt{(x + d)^2 + y^2}, \quad BP = \sqrt{(x - d)^2 + y^2}$$

and for a constant value of time delay

$$AP - BP = \sqrt{(x + d)^2 + y^2} - \sqrt{(x - d)^2 + y^2} = \text{const.} = l \text{ (say)}$$

where l is the difference between path lengths AP and BP. Simplifying, this equation may be put in the form

$$\frac{x^2}{a^2} - \frac{y^2}{b^2} = 1$$

where $\quad a^2 = \frac{l^2}{4}$ and $b^2 = d^2 - \frac{l^2}{4}$

This is the equation of a hyperbola, with foci at A and B. All the possible values of the delay t_d give a family of confocal hyperbolae (Note, however, that the delay can be either positive or negative but its magnitude cannot exceed $2d/c$, which is the delay at all the points on the line joining A and B, to the left of A and to the right of B). The determination of the delay locates the craft on one of these hyperbolae. If there is a third synchronized station C, the determination of the delays between the reception of signals from A and B and also between those from B and C would locate the craft on two hyperbolae, and their intersection gives the fix, as shown in Fig. 4.2. This

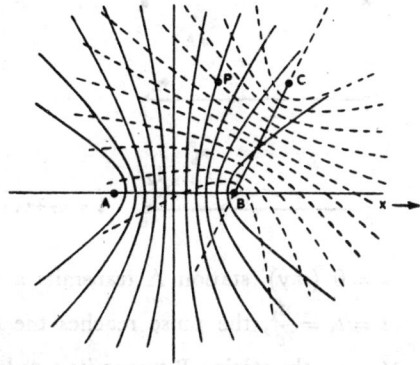

Fig. 4.2
Three stations producing two sets of hyperbolae

is the basic principle of hyperbolic navigational systems, in general. Different systems use different techniques for determining the delay. Two systems currently in use, namely LORAN and DECCA are described in the subsequent paragraphs.

4.1 Loran-A

Loran stands for 'Long range navigational aid'. This system was developed during the last war and found wide use. At present, certain regions of the world, principally the Pacific and Atlantic sea-boards of North America and the region around Japan are served by this facility. Loran-A or Standard

Loran as it was previously called, is the earlier version and operates in the higher MF band around 2 MHz. A subsequent development, called Loran-C, operates in a band around 100 kHz. These facilities can be used both by ships and by aircraft because of the nature of propagation in these frequency bands.

Loran is a pulse system. The ground stations transmit a train of pulses with a fixed time relation between them and at the receiver, these pulses are identified and the delay between them is measured on a cathode-ray tube. In the earlier paragraph, the example of two synchronized stations was given for simplicity. But if the transmitters at A and B transmit identical pulses simultaneously, there would be an ambiguity because it would not be possible to determine which pulse arrived first. To avoid this, the pulse transmissions are not made simultaneously. The station A (called the 'Master') transmits a pulse first and station B (called the 'Slave') transmits a pulse a fixed time after the reception of the pulse from A at B. The sequence of transmissions and receptions is indicated in Fig. 4.3. This is as follows:

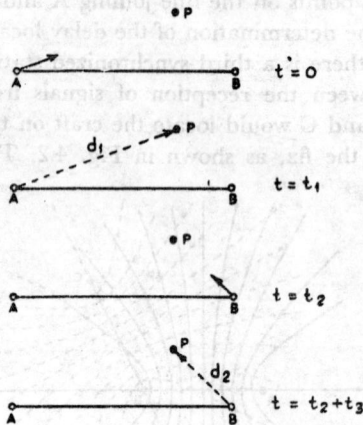

Fig. 4.3 The sequence of transmission and reception in Loran-A

$t = 0$ (say), station A transmits a pulse;

$t = t_1 = \dfrac{d_1}{c}$, the pulse reaches the craft;

$t = t_2$, the station B transmits a pulse (t_2 is called the 'absolute delay').

$t = t_2 + t_3 = t_2 + \dfrac{d_2}{c}$, the pulse from B reaches the craft. The transmission of B takes places after the pulse from A reaches B.

The time interval between the two received pulses, i.e. $t_2 + t_3 - t_1$, is measured. The fixed delay in the transmission of B, namely t_2, is known and, therefore, $t_3 - t_1$ can be determined. This quantity may be either positive or negative, whereas $t_2 + t_3 - t_1$ is always positive. The line AB is called the base line and in the case of Loran-A is from 400 to 700 km.

The pulse repetition frequencies used in the Loran system are in the region 20, 25, and $33\frac{1}{3}$ Hz, these rates being held constant to a high degree by crystal clocks. The sequence of pulses for a master-slave pair is ABAB...., the interval between the A's and B's being one pulse repetition period (T). The interval between one transmission of A and the next transmission of B is called 'absolute delay'. (The absolute delay must necessarily be greater than the time taken for the transmission to reach from A to B, i.e. $\dfrac{2d}{c} = \beta$). Let this be indicated by τ. Then the maximum interval between A and B pulses at the receiver is $\tau + \beta$, when the receiver is at a point on the line BA, beyond A, (such as R in Fig. 4.1) and the minimum delay is $\tau - \beta$, when it is at a point on the line AB, (such as S in Fig. 4.1). In order to avoid ambiguity in the identification of A and B pulses and aid measurement, the absolute delay is made more than half the repetition period $(T/2)$. Therefore, the interval between an A and the next B pulse is always greater than $T/2$. and the interval between a B pulse and the next A is always less than $T/2$. At the receiver, the pulses are displayed on an oscilloscope which has a special type of time-base [Fig. 4.4(a)], in which the period T is split into two parts, one half being displayed below the other. The spot moves from top left to top right, and flies back to bottom left in a period exactly equal to $T/2$. The duration of each trace is nearly $T/2$—actually $T/2$ less the flyback time. A and B pulses can thus be identified by their positions on the two traces. Fig. 4.4 illustrates the display when the pulses are in the correct position (a), and when they are in the wrong positions [(b) and (c)].

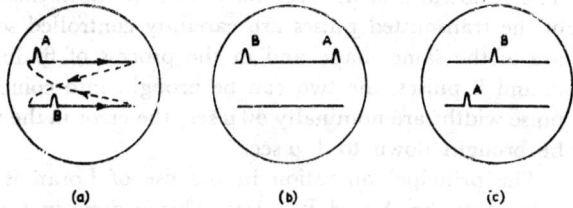

(a)   (b)   (c)

Fig. 4.4 Loran-A display. The correct display is shown in (a)

In order that the minimum interval between the receptions of A and B pulses should be greater than $T/2$, we should have

$$\tau - \beta > T/2, \text{ say } \tau - \beta = T/2 + \delta$$

where δ is some small delay which is arbitrarily fixed. The absolute delay τ is then

$$\tau = \frac{T}{2} + \beta + \delta$$

The maximum and minimum interval between the pulses are:

$$t_{max} = \left(\frac{T}{2} + \beta + \delta\right) + \beta = \frac{T}{2} + 2\beta + \delta$$

$$t_{min} = \left(\frac{T}{2} + \beta + \delta\right) - \beta = \frac{T}{2} + \delta$$

When the path lengths from the craft to A and B are the same, as for the points on the y-axis in Fig. 4.1, the interval between the received pulses is τ, the absolute delay.

4.2 Loran-A Equipment

Loran transmitters have a peak power of 100 kW which feed into a vertical quarter-wavelength antenna. The repetition rates of the pulses are accurately controlled by crystal clocks. The master station operates independently and transmits pulses of the required periodicity. The slave station is also provided with a crystal clock to maintain the repetition rate but the timing of these is controlled manually or semi-automatically to maintain the fixed delay.

The Loran system employs three basic repetition rates of 20 Hz, 25 Hz and $33\frac{1}{3}$ Hz. Each basic rate is sub-divided into a group of eight frequencies which differ from the above by small but accurately controlled steps of $\frac{1}{25}$, $\frac{1}{16}$ and $\frac{1}{8}$ Hz. Thus, on any single carrier frequency, there can be $3 \times 8 = 24$ channels. (The pulses from the station which has a different repetition frequency will move along the time-base and thus will not interfere with the station to which the receiver is synchronized). There are four carrier frequencies in the band 750-1950 kHz so that in all $24 \times 4 = 96$ channels are available.

The Loran receiver is a conventional superheterodyne receiver with one special feature—the gain of the receiver in the two parts of the time base (Fig. 4.4) are different and their relative values can be controlled manually. This permits the equalization of the A and B pulses to facilitate matching. The bandwidth of the receiver is 40 kHz. Both this bandwidth and the shape of the transmitted pulses are carefully controlled so that the received pulses are of the same shape and in the process of finding the delay between the A and B pulses, the two can be brought into coincidence. Thus, though the pulse widths are nominally 40 μ sec, the error in the measurement of delay can be brought down to 1 μ sec.

The principal operation in the use of Loran is the measurement of the delay between A and B pulses. This is done in the Loran indicator. In the earlier indicators, the time bases were controlled by crystals, which also gave calibration pulses. The measurement of the time interval followed a special procedure which involved the use of time bases of three speeds and a procedure for bringing the pulses into coincidence on the fastest time base. This took considerable time. In the modern receivers, the oscilloscope is still used to bring the pulses into coincidence by a delay control but the reading is obtained from an electronic counter which indicates the time difference in three decades.

4.3 Range and Precision of Standard Loran

As Loran operates in the upper MF band, both ground-wave and sky-wave receptions are possible. Ground-wave reception is operative mainly in the day and is particularly good over the sea. At night, both ground- and sky-wave receptions are possible, the latter being more prominent at long distances. For navigation, signals from at least two stations, but generally three stations, are necessary and, therefore, the factor of importance is the area over which usable signals are received from the pair or triplet of stations, rather than the maximum range at which the signal from a transmitter can be received. This area is dependent both on the maximum range of the stations and on the distance between the stations, or their 'base-line' as well as on the relative positions of the stations. In Fig. 4.5 are shown two Loran triplets and their

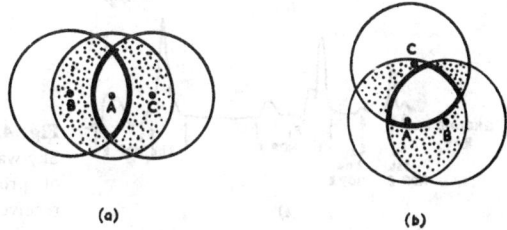

(a)   (b)

Fig. 4.5   Coverage of Loran-A chains

service area. The area within which a Loran fix can be obtained is shown heavily bounded and the areas where signals from only two stations can be obtained (providing only a hyperbolic line of position) is shown stippled. The service area depends on the latitude of the region, the season of the year and the time of the day. The average range for ground waves over the sea in the temperate latitudes is about 600 km and in equatorial regions about 500 km. The range over land is considerably less—about a half to a third of the above. Sky-wave ranges, which are the same over land and sea, may be appreciably higher.

The accuracy attainable with the Loran system is dependent on several factors. The first of these is the accuracy with which time interval measurements can be made, which in turn depends upon the signal strength. The second factor is the accuracy with which ground stations are synchronized. These two factors taken together may lead to a probable error of 1.5 to 2 μ sec in the measured time interval. Thirdly, errors may be introduced by sky-wave propagation, because the path taken by the wave is not along the ground but a longer one via the ionospheric layer. Fig. 4.6 shows the several possible paths which the wave can take via the ionosphere and the pulses these give rise to at the receiver. In addition to being delayed, the pulse appearing by the sky-wave path generally has a distorted shape which makes it difficult to match the waveforms of the pulses from two stations. However, with practice, an operator can identify and obtain the delay between two corresponding sky-waves (usually E_1 or E_2) and by averaging over a number of observations, reduce the measurement error to about 3 μ sec. Correction will still have to be applied for the additional delay introduced by the sky-wave path and curves and formulae based on average values of ionospheric heights, etc. are available for this purpose. However, they can be regarded as only approximate and so a further error is introduced into the computation of the delay.

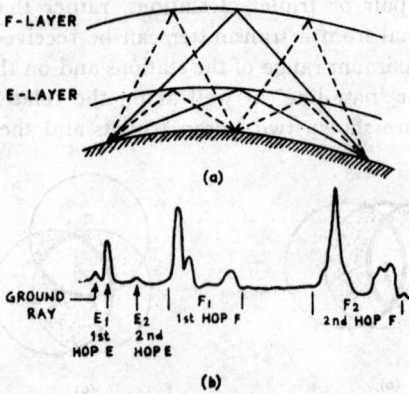

F-LAYER

E-LAYER

(a)

GROUND
RAY   E₁   E₂   F₁ 1st HOP F   F₂ 2nd HOP F
        1st   2nd
        HOP E HOP E

(b)

Fig. 4.6
Sky-wave reception of Loran-A signals [Paths of propagation are shown in (a) and the received signals in (b)]

The error in the determination of one time interval results in a corresponding uncertainty about the position of the hyperbola on which the craft is located. If t is the measured time interval and Δt is the probable error, the vehicle may be expected to be between the two hyperbolae corresponding to the delays at $t - \Delta t$ and $t + \Delta t$ as shown in Fig. 4.7(a). If a simultaneous measure-

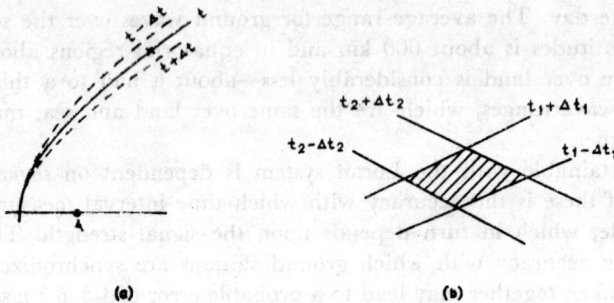

(a)

(b)

Fig. 4.7 Position errors in Loran-A navigation

ment of the interval between two stations in a chain gives a delay t_1 with an uncertainty Δt_1, and a delay t_2 with uncertainty Δt_2, the position of the craft will be within a quadrilateral area bounded by sections of four hyperbolic lines as in Fig. 4.7(b). If Δt_1 and Δt_2 are very small, the two hyperbolae defining the limits of the error are nearly parallel at the point of intersection. The region representing the uncertainty in fix is, therefore, a parallelogram (shown shaded in Fig. 4.7), the area of which increases as the angle between the two intersecting hyperbolae decreases. There is thus introduced a further geometrical factor into the errors in Loran. These considerations are, of course, common to all hyperbolic systems.

4.4 Loran-C

As stated earlier, Loran-C operates in the band 90-110 kHz. It is a
development arising out of war time work on low frequency Loran, operating
on 180 kHz. The advantage of the low frequency is that the range of ground
wave transmission is very much larger than at 2 MHz and attenuation is
nearly the same over land and over sea. The larger ground wave range, in
turn, permits greater separation between the master and the slave stations,
which is generally limited by the necessity to synchronize the two. With
a longer base line, a greater coverage can be obtained. The base-line lengths
for Loran-C can be between 1000-1800 km.

With the limited band-width available for Loran-C, the pulse has necessarily to be very long and this by itself would reduce the accuracy of the
system. However, greater accuracy than in Loran-A, is in fact attained by
matching the carrier frequency cycles within the pulse. To enable this to be
done, the carriers of the transmitters are synchronized and the pulse envelope
is standardized and accurately controlled. At the receiver, a match between
the pulse envelopes is obtained (to eliminate ambiguity) and simultaneously
the rf cycles within the pulse are matched. The time measurement accuracy
attainable thus becomes much greater than in Loran-A and in practice is of
the order of 0.1 μsec. The errors from this source are in fact smaller than the
errors introduced by the uncertainties and changes in the velocity of propagation of the ground wave. The travel time T between two points a distance D
apart is given by[16]

$$T = \frac{D}{v} + C_t$$

where v is the velocity of propagation of the ground wave and C_t is a correction
term introduced because of the finite conductivity of the ground and the
phase retardation introduced by it. The velocity v itself is related to the velocity
of electromagnetic waves in free space (c) by the equation:

$$v = c/n$$

where n is the refractive index of the medium, in this case, the atmosphere.
As the refractive index is subject to fluctuation and as the ground conductivity
is also not uniform, small uncertainties arise in the propagation time which
put a limit on the accuracy of fix obtainable with Loran-C.

The Loran-C receiver is fully automatic. The signal from the stations is
amplified and processed in two sections of the receiver, one handling the
envelope of the pulse and the other handling the rf pulse itself. Each section is
equipped with servo systems which operate on the sampled pulse. In the
envelope section, the delay is determined to about a microsecond and is
displayed on a digital display system. The cycle-matching section servo
matches the first three cycles of the rf pulse and displays the delay in units of
0.01 μsec. Cross-coupling between the two systems ensures unambiguous display
of delay or the time difference between master and slave pulses. This provision
of automatic search-and-track makes the receiver complex and sophisticated

and generally heavier than Loran-A receivers. The matching of the first few cycles of the pulse ensures that only ground-wave delay is determined and contamination by sky-wave which arrives approximately after 35 μsec is avoided. For details of the receiver operation see Ref. 16.

The Loran-C transmitters transmit pulses of long duration but of accurately controlled envelope which is so designed that 99% of the energy is contained within the band 90-110 kHz. The pulse repetition frequency is locked to the carrier frequency of 100 kHz so that all the pulses are of exactly the same shape in envelope and carrier. One such pulse is shown in Fig. 4.8. The peak

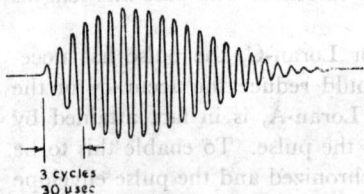

3 cycles
30 μsec

Fig. 4.8
Loran-C pulse

power is 1 MW. Actually, eight to nine pulses are transmitted in succession, and these are stored and combined in the receiver to improve the signal/noise ratio. The multiplicity of pulses also facilitates coding.

Loran-C has a range of 3500 km. over sea and 2200 km over land.

4.5 The Decca Navigation System

The Decca system operates in LF band (between 70 and 120 kHz) and employs unmodulated continuous waves. The measurement of the time difference in the reception of signals from two stations, which fixes the position on a hyperbola, is accomplished by measuring the phase difference between the signals of the two stations, the radiations of which are phase-locked, instead of the time interval between pulses, as in Loran. A decca chain consists of four stations, a master and three slaves, the latter being at the corners of a triangle and the former at the centre. These give three sets of hyperbolic position lines, one set corresponding to the master and each slave. Fix is obtained over a considerable area by the intersection of two hyperbolic lines.

If all the stations in a decca chain had the same frequency, their radiations will be indistinguishable at the receiver and the measurement of phase difference becomes impossible. This difficulty is avoided by radiating harmonically related frequencies from the four stations and making the phase measurements at a common harmonic frequency which is obtained at the receiver by using multiplying circuits. The result is the same as if the common harmonic were radiated by the stations, as will be shown. The four frequencies of the chain are related by a common sub-harmonic. If f is the sub-harmonic frequency, the master station has the frequency $6f$, and the slave stations the frequencies $5f$, $8f$ and $9f$. The master and each slave have, therefore, a common harmonic, as below.

Master station	*Slave*	*Common harmonic*
6f	(Red) 8f	24f
6f	(Purple) 5f	30f
6f	(Green) 9f	18f

The frequency f is about 14 kHz.

(The slave stations are distinguished by the colours which are used on the charts for the hyperbolic lines which they generate with the master station).

Referring to Fig. 4.1, let A be the master station, radiating a frequency $n_1 f$ and B the slave station radiating the frequency $n_2 f$. Let the radiation at A be proportional to $\cos 2\pi n_1 ft$ and that at B to $\cos 2\pi n_2 ft$. (The two radiations are phase-locked at a common harmonic frequency.) The field at P due to these two stations is proportional to $\cos (2\pi n_1 ft - \dfrac{2\pi(\overline{\mathrm{AP}})}{\lambda_1})$ and $\cos (2\pi n_2 ft$

$- \dfrac{2\pi(\overline{\mathrm{BP}})}{\lambda_1})$ where $\lambda_1 = c/n_1 f$ and $\lambda_2 = c/n_2 f$. Let the mth harmonic of the first and m_2th harmonic of the second be the same (i.e. $m_1 n_1 = m_2 n_2$). The outputs of the multipliers giving these harmonics are:

$$\cos m_1\left(2\pi n_1 ft - \frac{2\pi \overline{\mathrm{AP}}}{\lambda_1}\right)$$

and

$$\cos m_2\left(2\pi n_2 ft - \frac{2\pi \overline{\mathrm{BP}}}{\lambda^2}\right)$$

The phase difference between these two outputs is:

$$\frac{2\pi m_1 \overline{\mathrm{AP}}}{\lambda_1} - \frac{2\pi m_2 \overline{\mathrm{BP}}}{\lambda_2}$$

$$= \frac{2\pi m_1 n_1 f \,\overline{\mathrm{AP}}}{c} - \frac{2\pi m_2 n_2 f \,\mathrm{BP}}{c}$$

$$= \frac{2\pi \,\overline{\mathrm{AP}}}{c/m_1 n_1 f} - \frac{2\pi \,\overline{\mathrm{BP}}}{c/m_2 n_2 f} = \frac{2\pi}{\lambda_{mn}}(\overline{\mathrm{AP}} - \overline{\mathrm{BP}})$$

where $\qquad \lambda_{mn} = \dfrac{c}{m_1 n_1 f} = \dfrac{c}{m_2 n_2 f} = $ wavelength of the common harmonic frequency.

The phase difference measured is thus the same as if the stations radiated the common harmonic frequency.

The measurement of the phase difference rather than the time difference gives rise to ambiguity, as the phase difference can be measured without ambiguity only from 0 to 360°. A change in the path difference of λ_{mn} brings about a change in phase of 360°. Consider the line joining the master and a slave station. Movement along this line by $\dfrac{\lambda_{mn}}{2}$ brings about a change of phase of 360°. The half wavelength depends upon the particular master-slave pair and on the frequency, but has an average value of about 500 m. As the base line length may be 120 to 200 km, it is obvious that there will be several hundred phase changes of 360° in going from one station to another, which implies a very high degree of ambiguity. The phase measuring meter (Deco-meter) will do one complete revolution for each 360° phase change, and though another pointer may be geared to it so as to show the number of revolutions it has made, position determination becomes difficult unless one knows one's position very precisely at some time and can keep a continuous count of the revolutions of the decometer. The region defined by two adjacent hyperbolae which correspond to a phase change of 360° (i.e. a path difference change of λ_{mn}) is called a 'lane'. The transmitted frequencies, wavelengths and lane widths are given in Table 1 for $f = 14.166$ kHz.

Table 1
TYPICAL VALUES OF FREQUENCIES AND LANE WIDTH IN A DECCA SYSTEM

Station	Transmitted frequency kHz	Lane width on base line (m)	Common Harmonic Frequency kHz
Master	85.000 ($\lambda = 3521$ m)	—	—
Red slave	133.333 ($\lambda = 2640$ m)	440.074	340.00
Green slave	127.500 ($\lambda = 2347$ m)	586.765	255.00
Purple slave	70.833 ($\lambda = 4275$ m)	552.059	425.00

To reduce the ambiguity, the decca system employs a means of 'Lane identification'. This is done, in effect by measuring the phase difference between the signals from the stations at the frequency f (≈ 14.0 kHz). The hyperbolae defined by this are more widely spaced and on a base line, the distance between adjacent hyperbolae (corresponding to a phase change of 360°) is a half wavelength at the frequency f, i.e. about 10·5 km. The region between two adjacent hyperbolae is called a 'zone'. Each zone comprises a number of lanes. The number of lanes per zone, clearly, is equal to the ratio of the wavelengths of f and the common harmonic. These ratios are 24 (red), 18 (green) and 30 (purple). If the phase measurement is accurate to a hundredth of 360°, then the measurement of phase difference at f fixes the position within a fraction of the lane and so the particular lane within the zone can be determined with little probability of error. If one knows the position of the craft within about 5 km, then one can find the zone and the lane within the zone in which the craft is located. It must be realized, however, that even the zone may not be known with sufficient certainty, particularly in air navigation. A system of 'zone identification' has been introduced in the Mark X receiver and will be described later. Lane identification is called 'coarse fixing' and the determination of line of position within a lane is called 'fine fixing'.

The 14 kHz signal required for lane identification is provided by transmitting simultaneously from the master station the frequencies $6f$ and $5f$, and from each of the slaves in turn the frequencies $8f$ and $9f$. This is illustrated in Fig. 4.9. The lane identification signals are sent for short intervals thrice every minute, each time the master and one of the slaves making simultaneous

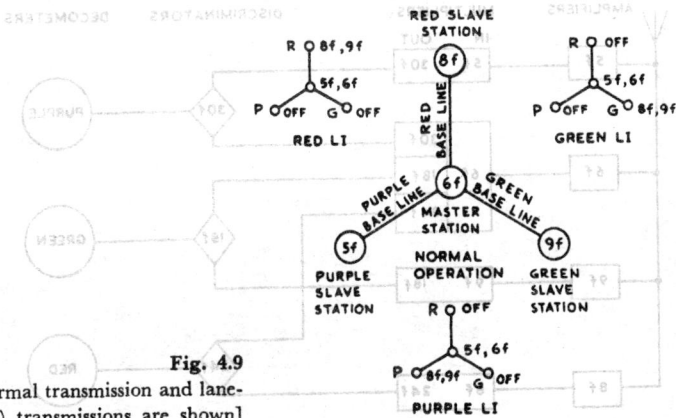

Fig. 4.9

A Decca chain [normal transmission and lane-
identification (LI) transmissions are shown]

transmissions. These transmissions are preceded by slight changes in the master
carrier frequency which actuates certain circuits in the receiver and changes
its configuration from that required for fine fixing to that required for lane
identification. The sequence is as follows. At the beginning of each full minute,
the normal transmissions are interrupted and the master station transmits
$6f - 60$ Hz, for 1/12 sec. This initiates the red lane identification cycle. Then
the master station transmits $6f$ and $5f$ and the red slave transmits $8f$ and $9f$,
for half a second. After this, normal transmission is resumed. At the beginning
of the 16th sec. the green lane identification is similarly initiated, the master
station in this case transmitting $6f + 60$ Hz and the green slave transmitting
$8f$ and $9f$ during this period. The normal transmission is then resumed and
interrupted at the beginning of the 30th sec. for purple lane identification.
The master station transmits $6f + 60$ Hz and $6f - 60$ Hz for 1/12 sec. followed
by $6f + 60$ Hz for 1/25 sec. Then the purple lane identification follows for
half a second. After this, for the rest of the complete minute, normal transmission is continued.

4.6 Decca Receivers

The block diagram of the decca receiver is shown in Figs. 4.10(a) and (b).
In Fig. 4.10(a), the receiver is in the configuration required for fine fixing.
The four frequencies received are separated by crystal filters, amplified, and
applied to frequency multipliers. The appropriate outputs of the multipliers
are given to the discriminators, the outputs of which are applied to the deco-
meters. These meters indicate the phase difference between the two inputs to
the discriminator and thus the position within the lane. Their rotors are
geared to indicators which give lane and zone also, which, of course, have
to be set initially to the correct figure. In Fig. 4.10(b), the receiver is shown in
the configuration for lane identification. The master frequencies $5f$ and $6f$,
and the slave frequencies $8f$ and $9f$ are amplified, and the two difference

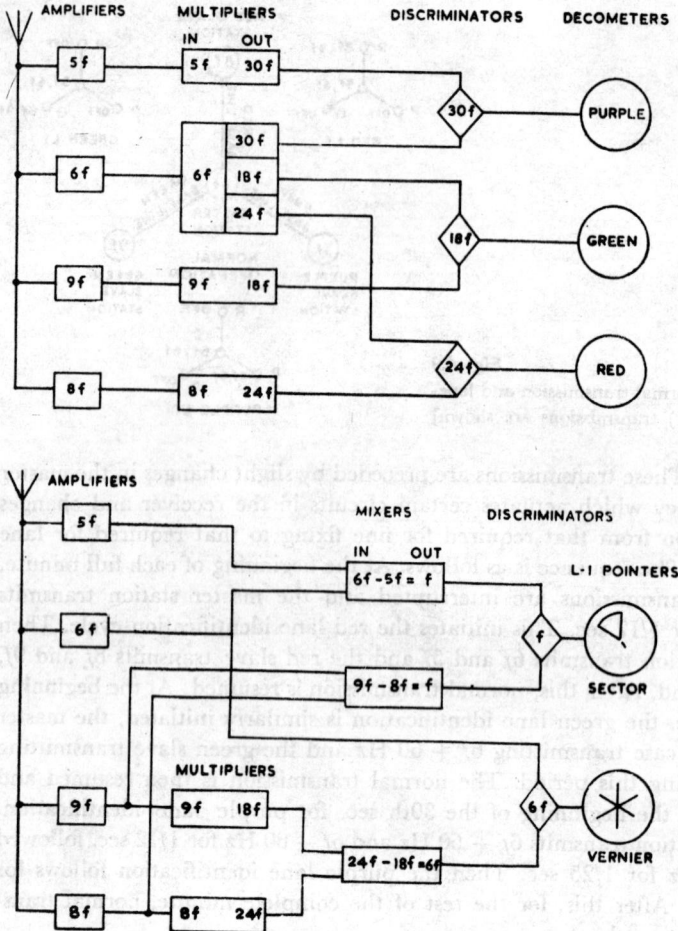

Fig. 4.10 Decca receiver configurations [(a) fine fixing, (b) lane identification]

frequencies obtained from mixer are applied to a discriminator and the output of the discriminator is applied to a decometer called the 'sector pointer'. This meter by itself could indicate the lane if it is sufficiently accurate, but to increase the accuracy, a $6f$ signal is extracted and applied to a second deco-meter. If fed straight to a decometer movement, this would give 6 rotations per zone and, therefore, 6 fold ambiguity. To resolve this, the 'vernier' move-ment is geared down in the ratio 1:6 and drives a 6-arm pointer. The sector pointer is mounted concentrically with the vernier and indicates which of the six pointers gives the correct lane. The width of the sector is made less than $\pi/3$, so that only one arm of the 6-arm pointer can be within it.

The block diagrams given in Fig. 4.10 pertain to the Mark V receiver which is used mainly in marine navigation. The accuracy which can be obtained with it is very high. It is not very suitable for use in aircraft, however, as they move too fast to utilize the accuracy to the full, and there is also the risk that lane integration may be lost. So a different receiver (Mark VII) has been designed for aircraft use, which obtains a coarser grid by making phase comparison at the frequencies of the slave stations, viz. $5f$, $8f$ and $9f$. To achieve this, the master station frequency is first reduced to f and then multiplied by 5,8 and 9 respectively for comparison with the transmissions of purple, red and green slaves. Thereby, the corresponding lanes become wider by factors of 6, 3 and 2 respectively. For further details, see Ref. 17.

The Mark X receiver, to which reference has been made, was developed to overcome two of the drawbacks of the other types of receivers which are met with in air navigation applications. The first of these, as mentioned earlier is the zone ambiguity. The second one relates to the difficulties experienced in lane identification at night over fairly long ranges. Multipath reception tends to introduce random phase-shifts which bring about fluctuations in the phasemeter indications. The effect of this on lane identification can be such as to give wrong lane indications. Both these drawbacks are overcome in Mark X receiver by employing special types of lane identification and zone identification signals. During the lane identification period, all the four frequencies $5f$, $6f$, $8f$ and $9f$ are momentarily radiated first by the master and then from the slaves. The received signals are brought to the same amplitude and added up in the receiver. This results in the formation of a train of pulses with recurrence frequency f (Fig. 4.11). The peak of this pulse, it has been shown[18],

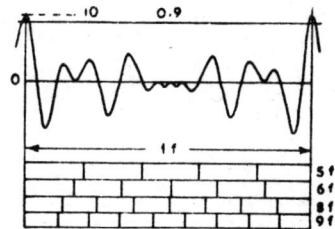

Fig. 4.11
Combined signals of 5f, 6f, 8f and 9f in Mark-X receiver

retains its correct time relation even when there is a considerable phase shift of the components. This pulse train is, therefore, made the basis of the lane identification scheme. It is made to control phase-locked sinusoidal oscillators which 'remember' the phase information from each station in turn and facilitate comparison of the phases at the frequency f. To enable zone identification, a transmission on the frequency $8 \cdot 2f$ is made along with the lane identification signal. This combines with the $8f$ signal in the receiver and the difference frequency $0 \cdot 2f$ is used to synchronize an oscillator of that frequency. The two signals derived from the master and slave stations are applied to a phase-measuring circuit to obtain the particular zone. The ambiguity is reduced by a factor of five by this means.

Air navigation has also necessitated automatic pictorial presentation of the position of the aircraft on a chart. Several models of 'flight-logs' have been developed to meet this requirement. Flight logs are automatic plotting devices which transfer the Decca receiver output on to a map display. The principles are described in literature,[19] and will not be dealt with here. In the flight log, the hyperbolic grid is transformed to a square one to simplify instrumentation of the recorder and, therefore, special distorted maps have to be used with them.

4.7 Range and Accuracy of Decca

The range of a Decca chain can be stated only when the probable error of location (circle of uncertainty) is specified. It also depends upon the distance between the master and the slave, the ground conductivity, etc. Ref. 14 may be seen for details. To quote one figure, for a radial error of 100 m, the range is about 300 km when the distance between the master and slave is 200 km. The instrumental errors in Decca are very small but variations of effective base line length, phase deviations introduced by skywave, etc. contribute the greater part of the error at long distances.

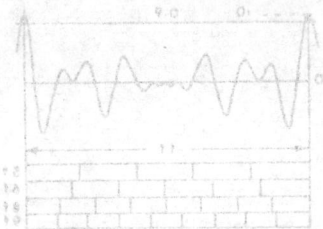

5

DME & TACAN

5.1 Distance Measuring Equipment

Both DME (distance measuring equipment) and TACAN (tactical air navigation) are secondary radar systems. The elements of such a system are shown in Fig. 5.1. The system consists of a pulse transmitter and receiver

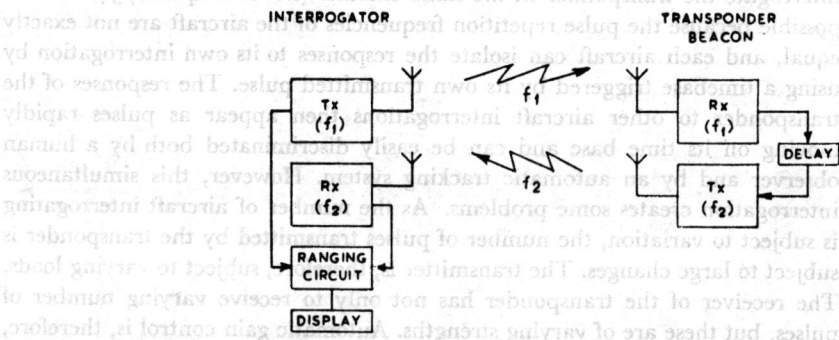

Fig. 5.1 Components of a secondary radar

(called the interrogator) carried in the craft and a pulse receiver-transmitter system (called the transponder) at a fixed position on the ground. The interrogator transmits rf pulses periodically at a frequency, say f_1. These are received by the receiver of the transponder, amplified, demodulated and made to trigger the transmitter, generally after a small fixed delay. The frequency of the transmitter, say f_2, is different from that of the receiver. In the craft, the receiver, which is tuned to f_2, receives these pulses and the delay between the transmitted and received pulses is measured to obtain the distance of the transponder from the craft. Both DME and TACAN work on this principle but a number of refinements are introduced to overcome some of the limitations of the basic system.

The DME and TACAN were developed at about the same time. The former was developed by the civil aviation authorities for use of civilian aircraft. The latter, was developed for the American Defence Services and was made public in 1955. While the DME provides only distance information, TACAN provides both distance and bearing (Rho-theta) with the same radiation. Civil aviation DME stations are usually supplemented by a VOR station at the same location, so that the two together provide rho-theta information for a suitably equipped aircraft. The frequencies of these two facilities are, however, in different frequency bands in contrast to the TACAN. The DME described here is identical in operation to the distance-measuring part of TACAN. (This is sometimes referred to as DME-T). Any aircraft equipped with DME equipment can make use of the range facility of TACAN and vice versa. We will first describe the DME and later show how the equipment is modified to provide bearing as in TACAN.

5.1 Distance Measuring Equipment

Before going into the details of the refinements in the DME, some of the problems of the simple secondary radar (Fig. 5.1) must be appreciated. One of the features of the pulsed secondary radar is that a number of aircraft can interrogate the transponder in the same channel (i.e. at frequency f_1). This is possible because the pulse repetition frequencies of the aircraft are not exactly equal, and each aircraft can isolate the responses to its own interrogation by using a timebase triggered by its own transmitted pulse. The responses of the transponder to other aircraft interrogations then appear as pulses rapidly moving on its time base and can be easily discriminated both by a human observer and by an automatic tracking system. However, this simultaneous interrogation creates some problems. As the number of aircraft interrogating is subject to variation, the number of pulses transmitted by the transponder is subject to large changes. The transmitter is, therefore, subject to varying loads. The receiver of the transponder has not only to receive varying number of pulses, but these are of varying strengths. Automatic gain control is, therefore, used. In the interrogator receiver too, the number of pulses will vary with the number of interrogating aircraft, but their strengths are equal as they emanate from the same transponder. Automatic gain control is used in this case also. The use of automatic gain control introduces some problems. In the transponder, it prevents the response to weak signals when there are a large number of aircraft. In the interrogator, the variation of gain might prevent the reception of responses to its own interrogation. Both these disadvantages are overcome by operating the transponder at a constant pulse rate which is independent of the number of aircraft interrogating. This is called the 'constant duty cycle operation' (The duty cycle is the fraction of the time that the transmitter is on).

Another drawback in the simple system is that when very few aircraft are interrogating, the gain of the receiver in the transponder goes up and some noise pulses may trigger the transmitter.

In the DME, constant duty cycle operation is achieved by making the noise pulses trigger the transponder transmitter at a constant rate. When interrogations are received, these replace the noise pulses and keep the duty ratio constant. With the maximum number of aircraft interrogating, the gain of the receiver is reduced slightly so that the only pulses transmitted are the responses to interrogation. It requires only a small change of receiver gain to bring this about.

5.2 Operation of DME

5.2.1 DME Transmissions

The DME interrogator operates in the band 1025-1150 MHz with 126 channels spaced 1 MHz apart. The transponder operates in the band 962-1213 MHz. For each channel, a pair of frequencies (f_1 and f_2) which differ by 63 MHz are allotted. The frequency of 63 MHz is used as the intermediate frequency in the receivers.

Both the interrogator and transponder operate with pulse pairs consisting of two pulses 12 μsec apart. The reason for using pulse pairs instead of single pulses is that thereby, the probability of the transponder triggering to spurious noise pulses is reduced. The gain of the receiver may, therefore, be maintained at a high level. The pulse rate in the transponder is about 3000 pulse pairs per second. This rate is kept constant, as explained above, so that noise pulse-pairs trigger the transmitter in the absence of interrogation pulses. These additional noise-actuated pulses are called 'filler pulses'. In order that pulses trigger the transponder transmitter, they should satisfy two conditions, viz. (a) two pulses must be received 12 μsec apart, and (b) both pulses must have amplitudes exceeding the triggering level.

The pulses received from the interrogator invariably satisfy the first condition, as they are double pulses with 12 μsec separation. The signals are generally above the triggering level (if they are within a certain range) so that the second is also satisfied. But only some noise pulses satisfy these conditions, and the number that do so depends upon the triggering level. By adjusting this, the required number of filler pulses can be obtained. Fig. 5.2 illustrates how the response and filler pulses are generated in the transponder receiver. Fig. 5.2(a) shows the trace of the video output of the receiver, in which A is the interrogation from an aircraft and the rest are noise pulses. The pulse pairs B,C,D,E and F, arising from noise, satisfy the conditions (a) and (b) above. The pulse G and the pulse pair H do not trigger the transmitter as they do not satisfy the conditions (a) and (b) respectively. Fig. 5.2(b) shows the output of the trigger circuit and Fig. 5.2(c) the pulse pairs generated by these, which in turn modulate the transmitter. These pulse pairs have the required 12 μsec separation and each pulse is of 3·5 μsec duration. The noise-generated pulses are irregularly spaced in time and are said to have 'squitter'.

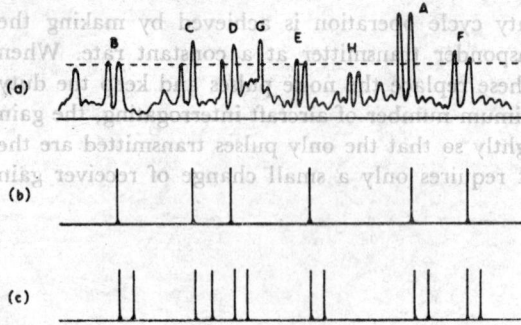

Fig. 5.2 Generation of response and filler pulses in the transponder receiver [(a) receiver output, (b) single pulses generated by pulse-pairs, (c) pulse-pairs generated by these]

5.2.2 Air-borne DME Interrogator

The block diagram of the interrogator is shown in Fig. 5.3. The transmitter rf chain consists of a crystal oscillator giving one of 126 frequencies around

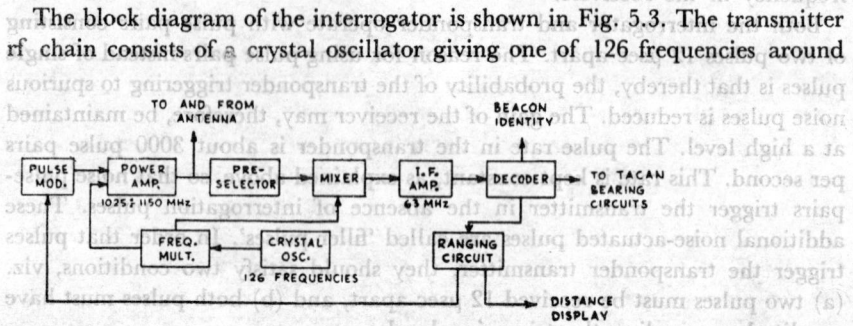

Fig. 5.3 Block diagram of airborne DME interrogation

45 MHz, a frequency multiplier and a power amplifier. The output power ranges from 50W to 1 kW depending on the type of equipment. The power amplifier is modulated by a pulse modulator which is timed by wave-forms obtained from the ranging circuit. A common antenna is used for the receiver and transmitter. The transmitted energy is prevented from getting into the receiver by selective elements in the transmission line which act as wave-traps for the transmitter frequency. A part of the oscillator output is mixed with the incoming signal and because of the 63 MHz separation between the transmitted and received frequencies, an intermediate frequency of 63 MHz is generated. This is amplified, demodulated and applied to the ranging circuit. This circuit tracks the received signal and converts the delay into a distance display.

The receiver has two modes of operation, the search mode and the tracking mode. Initially in the search mode, the transmitter operates at a pulse repetition frequency of 150 pulses/sec. The waveforms of the tracking circuit are shown in Fig. 5.4 which shows the transmitter pulse (a), the variable delay (b), and the gate wave-form (c). The output of the demodulator (video pulse

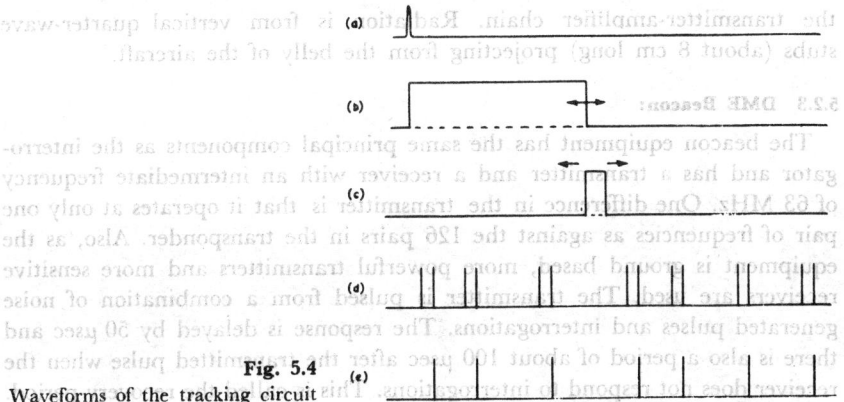

Fig. 5.4
Waveforms of the tracking circuit

pairs) is shown in (d) and the single pulse generated from them in (e). The operation of the tracking circuit is as follows. The transmitter pulses trigger a delay circuit which in turn triggers the short duration (20 μsec) gate pulse generator. The delay is variable and is increased gradually from zero to a maximum of about 2400 μsec by a motor driven potentiometer, thereby moving the gating pulse from left to right. This search may take about 20 sec. The output pulse pairs of the receiver are converted to single pulses and applied to a circuit which is gated by the wave-form shown in Fig. 5.4(c). As the gating pulse moves to the right, it allows the pulses which coincide with it in time to pass into a counter circuit. As long as these pulses are un-synchronized squitter pulses, the number of them passing the gate in a given time is small. This number can be calculated as follows. As there are 150 gate periods per second, each of 20 μsec duration, the gate is open for a total period of 3000 μsec sec. On the average there are 3000 pulses/sec received from the beacon and so in 3000 μsec about 9 pulses are received. On the other hand, as the gate pulse passes the relatively stationary response pulses, the rate increases suddenly. To calculate this, we have to assume a search rate. Taking this as 100 μsec/sec. (i.e. approximately 10 miles per sec in range), the gate pulse takes 20/100 or 1/5 second to pass a distance equal to its width. In this time, 30 pulses of the response appear in the gate. This sudden increase in the number of pulses (from 9 to 30) actuates circuits which terminate the search mode and put the receiver in the track mode. The pulse repetition frequency of the interrogator is then reduced to about 25 pulses/sec and the 20 μsec gate follows the desired response. If the reply falls in the early part of the gate, it advances. If it falls in the later part, the gate is delayed. A low inter-rogation rate is possible in the track mode since the possible change in the position of the aircraft is quite small in one interpulse period.

The position of the aircraft, indicated by the delay of the gating pulse is displayed either in analog or digital form. Accuracies of 150 m are commonly achieved. The air-borne equipment is nowadays transistorized except for the transmitter-amplifier chain. Radiation is from vertical quarter-wave stubs (about 8 cm long) projecting from the belly of the aircraft.

5.2.3 DME Beacon:

The beacon equipment has the same principal components as the interrogator and has a transmitter and a receiver with an intermediate frequency of 63 MHz. One difference in the transmitter is that it operates at only one pair of frequencies as against the 126 pairs in the transponder. Also, as the equipment is ground based, more powerful transmitters and more sensitive receivers are used. The transmitter is pulsed from a combination of noise generated pulses and interrogations. The response is delayed by 50 μsec and there is also a period of about 100 μsec after the transmitted pulse when the receiver does not respond to interrogations. This is called the recovery period. Some interrogations are consequently lost but the amount of these is typically of the order of 20%.

The beacon transmits identification signals for a period of 3 sec once every 37 sec. The identification is in the form of regularly spaced pulses at 1350 pulse pairs per sec. During this period, the normal chain of random pulses are suppressed. The identification, which is in the form of a 3 letter morse code, activates a tuned circuit in the aircraft. The ranging circuit is kept in the previously registered position.

5.3 TACAN

TACAN, as stated earlier, provides both range and bearing information with the same radiation. The operation is conveniently divided into the range facility and the bearing facility. The operation of the range facility is precisely the same as in DME. The bearing information is provided by a method which is similar in principle to that used in the VOR. The antenna radiation has a cardioid polar diagram which is made to rotate at 15 rev/sec and provides a variable phase signal in the form of amplitude modulation of the pulse train. In the place of the reference sinusoid employed in the VOR, a distinctive group of pulses is radiated every time the maximum of the cardioid passes East (90°). This pulse group is a precisely regulated one, consisting of 12 pulses, each a 12 μsec twin, spaced exactly 30 μsec apart. A special pulse group decoder separates this in the air-borne equipment. The delay between a chosen datum point (say, the zero-crossing) of the variable phase signal and the marker pulse is computed and displayed in a bearing indicator.

The accuracy obtainable by this method is insufficient for the precision aimed at in TACAN, and a special technique is used to increase the accuracy. A nine-lobe pattern is superposed on the cardioid, making the combined radiation pattern appear as in Fig. 5.5(a). This pattern has a fixed phase relation to the cardioid, one maximum of the nine lobe pattern coinciding with the maximum of the cardioid. The rotation of this antenna pattern at 15 rev/sec gives a signal which has a modulation of 15 Hz and 135 Hz. Phase comparison

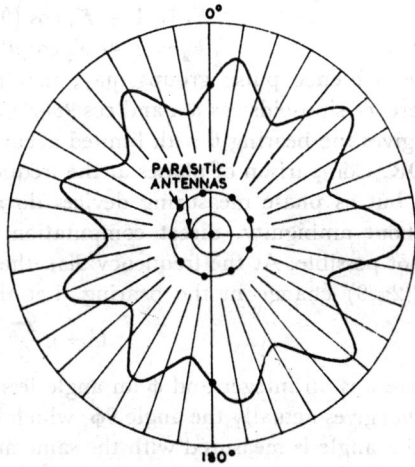

(a)

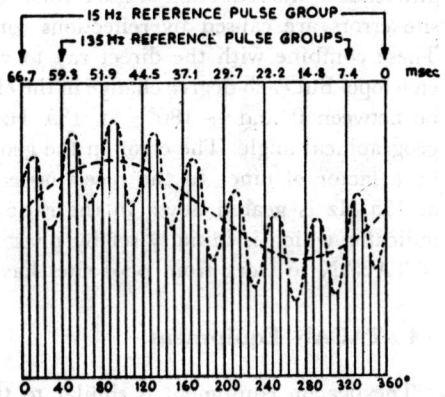

(b)

Fig. 5.5
TACAN radiation pattern [(a) polar diagram, (b) pulse sequence at the receiver]

is made at both the frequencies, and as will be shown below, phase comparison at 135 Hz increases the accuracy nine-fold. As a reference for phase comparison at 135 Hz, a group of pulses consisting of six 12 μsec twins with a spacing of 24 μsec is radiated at the zeros of the 135 Hz sinusoid. Eight of these reference groups are transmitted for every rotation, the ninth position being taken by the group for 15 Hz modulation (Fig. 5.5(b)).

The field pattern of the TACAN beacon may be expressed by the equation:

$$\varepsilon(t) = A + B \cos(\theta - \omega_s t) + C \cos 9\,(\theta - \omega_s t)$$

where $\varepsilon(t)$ is the field at the receiving point, situated in the direction corresponding to θ; A, B, C are constants and ω_s is the angular velocity of pattern rotation ($2\pi \times 15$ radians/sec). On demodulation of the pulse train, two sinusoids are obtained:

$$E_1 = 1 + K_1 \cos (\theta - \omega_s t)$$

and
$$E_2 = 1 + K_2 \cos 9(\theta - \omega_s t)$$

The reference pulse groups may, in effect, be regarded as providing the reference sinusoids $\cos \omega_s t$ and $\cos 9\omega_s t$. Comparison of phases at the frequency ω_s gives the bearing θ with limited accuracy but without ambiguity, as in the VOR. Comparison of phases at the frequency $9\omega_s$ would give the phase angle 9θ, but as phase measuring devices do not measure angles greater than 2π without ambiguity, direct computation of θ from this phase measurement is not possible. At the frequency $9\omega_s$, there is a phase change of 2π for every $40°(2\pi/9)$ change in the bearing. Let the bearing be expressed as follows:

$$\theta = n \frac{2\pi}{9} + \phi$$

where n is an integer and ϕ an angle less than $2\pi/9$. The phase measurement at $9\omega_s$ gives actually the angle 9ϕ, which has some value between zero and 2π. If this angle is measured with the same accuracy as the phase of ω_s, the error in 9ϕ is the same as the error in θ and so the error in ϕ is reduced by a factor of 9. The bearing is computed as the sum of an integral multiple of $2\pi/9$ and ϕ, and thus the accuracy is the same as in the measurement of ϕ. This technique also leads to the reduction of site errors. As was stated in Chapter 3 Sec. 3.4(b), site errors are caused by reflections (or re-radiations) from nearby objects. These combine with the direct ray to change the phase of the modulation envelope. But each degree change in the electrical angle (which must necessarily be between 0 and $\pm 180°$) at 135 Hz corresponds to $\frac{1}{9}°$ change in the geographical angle. The error in the geographical angle is, therefore, reduced by a factor of nine. In the receiving equipment, the phase angle measured at 135 Hz is geared down in the ratio 9:1 and connected to the bearing indicator which is initially set by phase measurement at 15 Hz. The ability of TACAN to work from poor sites has led to its use on ships.

5.4   TACAN Equipment

The beacon equipment is similar to the DME except for the provision of the synchronizing pulse groups. The block diagram is shown in Fig. 5.6. The antenna is common to the receiver and transmitter and a duplexer is employed to ensure that the receiver and transmitter are isolated. The duplexers consist of tuned cavities which reject the undesired signal. The antenna of TACAN differs from that of the DME as the equipment has to provide bearing information. The radiator is made up of a stack of discone antennas.[13] Around this are two coaxial plastic cylinders in which parasitic elements are embedded. The inner cylinder which has a diameter of about 15 cm has one parasitic element and the outer cylinder of diameter about 90 cm has nine parasitic elements. These modify the horizontal radiation pattern of the antenna (as shown in Fig. 5.5), which would otherwise be circular, by superposing on it two sinusoidal variations, having one cycle and nine cycles respectively. The two cylinders are rotated together at 900 rev/min by a speed controlled motor.

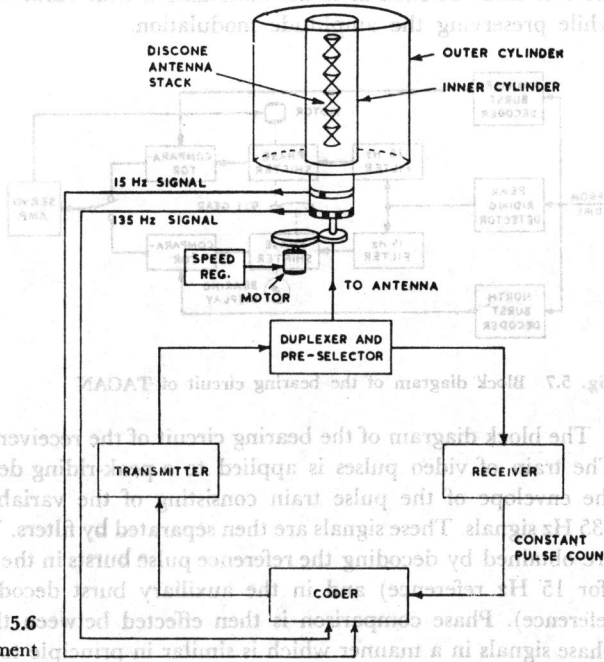

Fig. 5.6
TACAN beacon equipment

The discone radiators have a broad-band to accommodate the range of frequencies (960-1215 MHz) employed. The stack of radiators typically gives a vertical polar diagram, which has a maximum at an angle of 5° above the horizon.

A disc of non-ferrous metal is coupled to the rotating cylinders. Embedded in this are two sets of soft-iron slugs, nine in one set and one in the other. As these pass over a magnetic coil system, they give rise to a pulse, which is made to generate the groups of timing pulses from which reference sinusoids are generated in the TACAN receiver. One of these pulse groups which gives a reference for the 15 Hz modulation, is emitted when the maximum of the antenna pattern is pointing East, and consists of 24 pulses, the spacing between pulses being alternately 12 and 18 μsec. There is one such group for every revolution. The 135 Hz reference pulse group is emitted eight times per second (the ninth group coincides with 15 Hz reference and is suppressed). These pulse groups consist of 12 pulses spaced 12 μsec apart. When reference pulses are radiated, the normal constant-duty cycle pulses are omitted. Provision is also made for an identity pulse group to be emitted as in DME beacons.

TACAN air-borne equipment—This comprises the DME interrogator to which the bearing facility has been added. The block diagram of Fig. 5.3 is, therefore, applicable as far as the range facility is concerned. The output to the bearing circuitry is taken from the decoder. Automatic gain control of the DME receiver must be such as to accommodate a wide variation of the input signal while preserving the amplitude modulation.

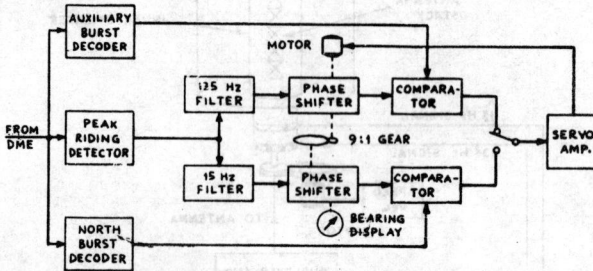

Fig. 5.7   Block diagram of the bearing circuit of TACAN

The block diagram of the bearing circuit of the receiver is shown in Fig. 5.7. The train of video pulses is applied to a peak-riding detector which extracts the envelope of the pulse train consisting of the variable phase 15 Hz and 135 Hz signals. These signals are then separated by filters. The reference signals are obtained by decoding the reference pulse bursts in the North burst decoder (for 15 Hz reference) and in the auxiliary burst decoder (for the 135 Hz reference). Phase comparison is then effected between the variable and fixed phase signals in a manner which is similar in principle to that employed in the VOR receiver. This function is performed by a servo system which reduces the phase difference between the two signals to zero by servo driven phase-shifter. A single motor drives the two phase shifters, but there is reduction gear of 9:1 ratio between the two. The error signal may be obtained either from the 15 Hz loop or the 135 Hz loop. Whenever the 135 Hz signal is present and the phase error is less than $\pm 20°$ in the 15 Hz chain, the 135 Hz loop takes over (i.e. the switch S is moved up). If the 135 Hz signal is absent or the phase error in the 15 Hz chain is more than $\pm 20°$, the 15 Hz loop is completed (switch S moves down). By this means, ambiguity (which phase comparison at 135 Hz entails) is eliminated. The bearing is typically displayed on a compass-type indicator. The TACAN receiver, in its modern version is typically transistorized.

6
Aids to Approach & Landing

THE FLIGHT of an aircraft culminates in a landing at an airport. While approaching the airport, the aircraft takes a path in line with the runway and from a certain distance begins to descend until it touches the ground at a point near the runway threshold. When visibility is good, whether in the day or at night, this operation is carried out by visual observation of the ground and the landing lights, etc. The landing is then performed under 'visual flight rules (VFR)' conditions. Usually this is taken to indicate a horizontal visibility of 5 km or more and vertical visibility or ceiling of 300 m. When these conditions are not satisfied, the landing is under 'Instrument flight rules (IFR)' conditions.

Special aids are provided at airports to enable the aircraft to execute landings under bad visibility. Such aids have to provide information to the aircraft about its exact position in relation to a desired path of descent. This implies that information both about any deviation of the position in the vertical and horizontal positions of the aircraft is to be given.

Two types of aids will be dealt with here—the instrument landing system (ILS) and the ground controlled approach (GCA). There is a fundamental operational difference between these two. The former presents the pilot with information about his position in relation to a prescribed approach path, continuously, by an instrument carried in the aircraft. The GCA (or more particularly, its component, the precision approach radar), employs operators on the ground who determine the position of the aircraft and instruct the pilot on the course he is to follow, i.e. they exercise control, through the pilot, on the movement of the aircraft. Clearly, this facility does not require the aircraft to carry any special navigational equipment. Only a communication set, which is required even for other purposes, is needed in the aircraft. A brief description of the two systems is given below.

6.1 Instrument Landing System

The Instrument Landing System (ILS) comprises the units localizer, glide-path (or glide-slope) and marker beacons (Fig. 6.1). The localizer defines a vertical equi-signal plane which passes over the centre line of the

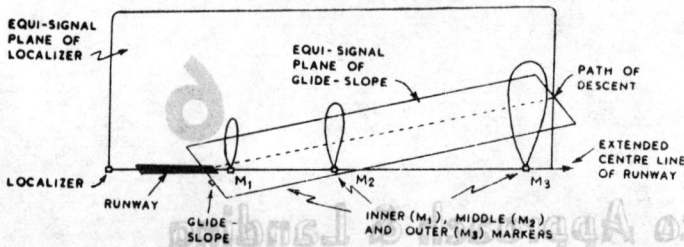

Fig. 6.1 Location of the components of the instrument landing system (ILS) with respect to the runway

runway and the glide-slope, an equi-signal plane inclined to the horizontal at the desired angle of descent, generally between 2° and 4°. The intersection of these two planes gives the approach path. Three marker beacons are also installed at certain specified distances from the end of the runway. They give an indication in the aircraft as it flies over them and thereby help the pilot to check his position in the approach path.

(a) The Localizer

The localizer operates in the VHF band (108-110 MHz) and consists of a transmitter with an antenna system, the radiation of which has two lobes, one with a predominant modulation of 90 Hz and the other with a predominant modulation of 150 Hz, as shown in Fig. 6.2(c). Along the line marked XOX', the two signals are equal and this equi-signal course is aligned with the centre line of the runway.

The antenna array by means of which this pattern is obtained consists of seven, or sometimes eight, Alford loops, placed on a line at right angles to the extended centre line of the runway and about a 300 m from the end of the runway. These loops make up three arrays, two of the three loops each on either side and the remaining one (or two) in the centre. The former are called side-band loops and the latter the carrier antenna. The carrier, modulated to the same depth by sinusoids of 90 Hz and 150 Hz, is fed to the central antenna, which has a polar diagram as shown in Fig. 6.2(a). To the other two arrays, only the side-bands of 90 Hz and 150 Hz modulation are supplied. At the same time, the following phase relations of the side-band with respect to those of the central antenna are established and maintained.

(a) The 150 Hz side-bands are reversed in phase with respect to those in the central antenna.

(b) The side-bands of both the modulating signals are phase shifted by 90°

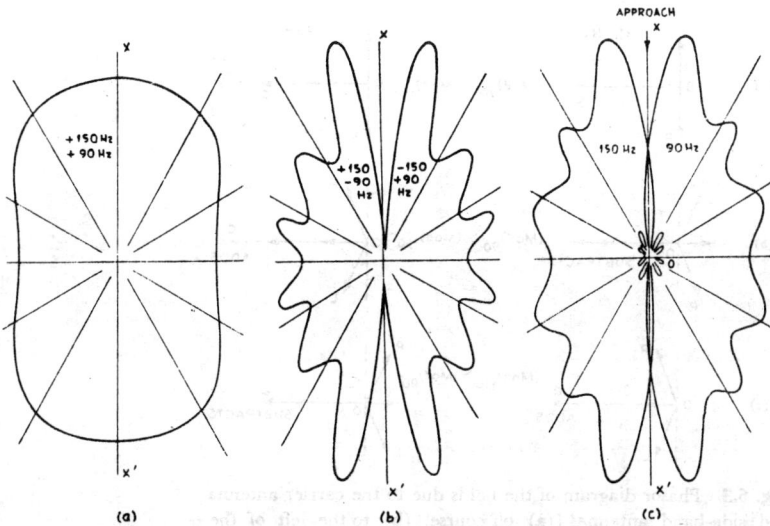

Fig. 6.2 Polar diagrams of the localizer [(a) carrier antenna, (b) side-band antennas, (c) the combined pattern; note the minor lobes generated by the array]

(c) The side-band power is split into two equal parts and fed to the two side-band arrays, but a phase-shift of 180° is introduced into one of them.

In addition, the spatial arrangement of the loops is designed to give a polar diagram of the 'butterfly' type shown in Fig. 6.2(b). As a result of the phase relations given above, the fields produced by the two side-band antennas at a distant point are in phase quadrature to that produced by the central one, in addition to being mutually in anti-phase. At any point along the line XOX', the fields cancel, as the two antennas radiate in anti-phase and the path lengths are equal. There is thus a null along this line. On either side of it, the fields will not cancel as the path lengths are different and the resultant field is the phasor sum of the two. The combined field pattern of the central and side-band antennas is as shown in Fig. 6.2(c) and has 90 Hz modulation predominant on one side and 150 Hz modulation on the other. The manner in which this arises is explained below with the aid of the phasor diagrams in Fig. 6.3. Only the side-band phasors are represented for the sake of clarity, those of 150 Hz modulation on the left and those of 90 Hz modulation on the right.

Fig. 6.3(a) represents the situation along the line XOX'. OC is the phasor of the field due to the central antenna, and OR and OL these due to the side-band antennas on the right and left of the central antenna. OR and OL are in phase quadrature to OC and mutually in phase opposition. As they are equal, they cancel, leaving only the central antenna field. The same applies to the 150 Hz side-band signal, as shown on the right. Note, however, that the phasors OR and OL are reversed in position. This can be brought about

(a) L 150 Hz 0 ⊢———→ C $(Mod)_{90} = (Mod)_{150}$ R 90 Hz 0 ⊢———→ C L

(b) L C 0 SUBTRACTS R $(Mod)_{90} > (Mod)_{150}$ ADDS R 0 ⊢— ∞ - -→ C L

(c) R 0 ⊢———→ C ADDS L $(Mod)_{150} > (Mod)_{90}$ R 0 C SUBTRACTS L

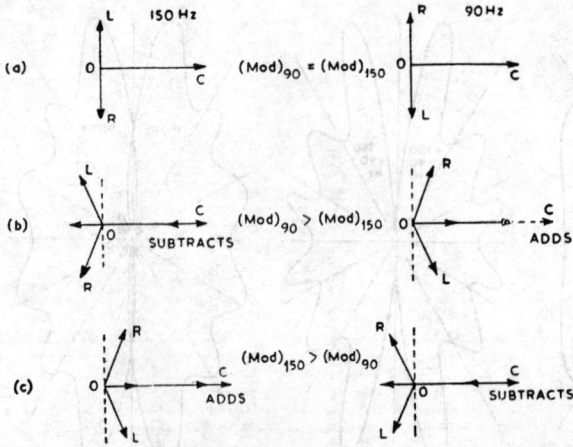

Fig. 6.3 Phasor diagram of the fields due to the carrier antenna and side-band antennas [(a) on course, (b) to the left of the course, (c) to the right of the course]

either by the reversal of the modulating signal of 150 Hz in the side-band generators in electronically modulated equipment or by introducing a phase shift of 180° in the side-band signal in mechanically modulated equipment.

In Fig. 6.3(b), the situation on the left hand side of the centre line is shown. The signal from one antenna (OL) is phase advanced and that from the other (OR), phase retarded by the same amount. In the case of 90 Hz modulation, the two phasors give a resultant which adds to the signal from the central antenna. The same phase changes, in the case of the 150 Hz modulation give a resultant which subtracts from the 150 Hz phasor of the central antenna. The 90 Hz modulation thus predominates on the left hand side. Similarly it is shown in Fig. 6.3(c) that the 150 Hz modulation predominates on the right hand side.

The means by which the modulation is brought about depends upon the type of equipment. This may be done either electronically or by mechanical means.[13] In the earlier models and also in some later ones, mechanical modulation is employed in the manner explained below. The antenna system and the modulators are shown in Fig. 6.4. The signal from the transmitter is divided into two parts by the modulation bridge ABCD and goes by two paths to the antenna bridge EFGH. Modulation at 90 Hz and 150 Hz is achieved by mechanical modulators. These consist of two quarter-wave transformers coupled to the lines BE and DG. One end of the quarter-wave line is short-circuited and the other end terminated by two plates in the centre of which is a specially shaped plate rotated by the motor M. The plate in the BE branch has three and the one in the DG branch has five lobes. The rotation of these plates presents a varying impedance across the line and, therefore, changes the power transmitted in the lines. The motor rotates at

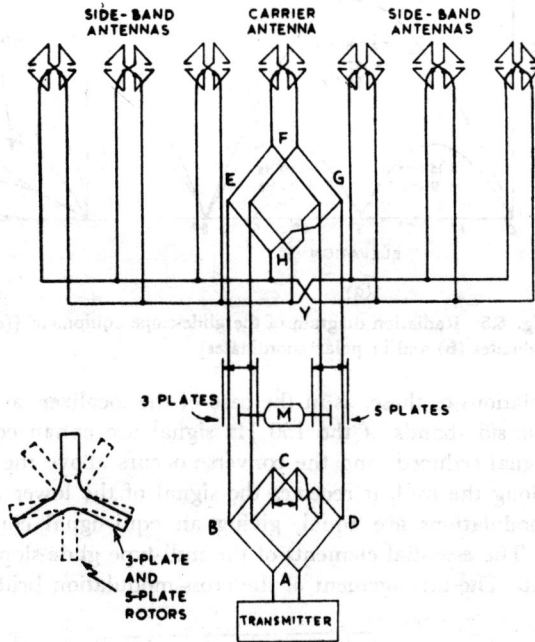

SIDE-BAND ANTENNAS   CARRIER ANTENNA   SIDE-BAND ANTENNAS

3 PLATES   M   5 PLATES

C

3-PLATE AND 5-PLATE ROTORS   B   D   A

TRANSMITTER

Fig. 6.4
Localizer antenna array

1800 rev/min., producing modulation at 90 Hz and 150 Hz. The plates are shaped to obtain sinusoidal modulation. The bridge, in one arm (CD) of which a phase change of 180 is introduced, ensures that the modulations on the two sides do not interact.

At the antenna bridge, the carrier + 90 Hz side-bands from E and the carrier + 150 Hz side-bands from G add at F and go to the central antenna, which, therefore, radiates the carrier and all the side-bands. Power comes to H also from two paths, EH and GH, but owing to the transposition at X, the carriers cancel and the 150 Hz side-band frequencies get reversed. The power at this point divides into the two paths going to the two side-band arrays and the phase reversal of one is brought about by the transposition at Y. Phase quadrature of side-band radiations is accomplished by introducing additional lengths of transmission lines.

(b) Glide-Slope System

The principle of operation of the glide-slope currently in use, called the null-type glide-slope is very similar to that of the localizer. The system, which operates in the band 339·3-335 MHz employs two antennas, which have vertical polar diagrams as shown in Fig. 6.5. The larger lobe, representing the radiation from the lower antenna has the carrier and the side-bands of 90 Hz and 150 Hz in equal strength. The two smaller lobes represent the radiation from the top antenna and have only the side-band frequencies. The phase

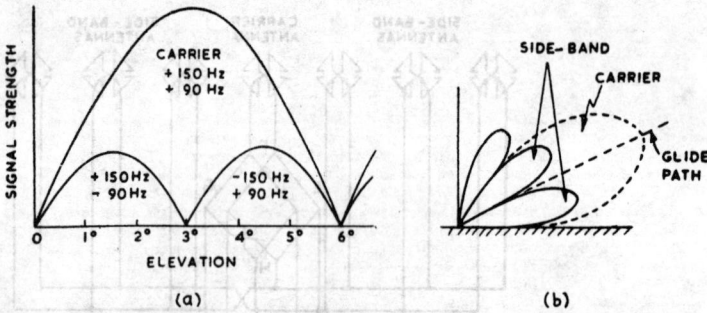

Fig. 6.5 Radiation diagram of the glide-slope equipment [(a) in cartesian co-ordinates (b) and in polar coordinates]

relations of these, as in the case of the localizer, are such that below the null, the side-bands of the 150 Hz signal are enhanced and those of the 90 Hz signal reduced, and the converse occurs above the null. If the aircraft flies along the null, it receives the signal of the lower antenna only, and the two modulations are equal, giving an equi-signal course.

The essential elements of the null-type glide-slope system are shown in Fig. 6.6. The arrangement of the cross-modulation bridge and the antenna bridge

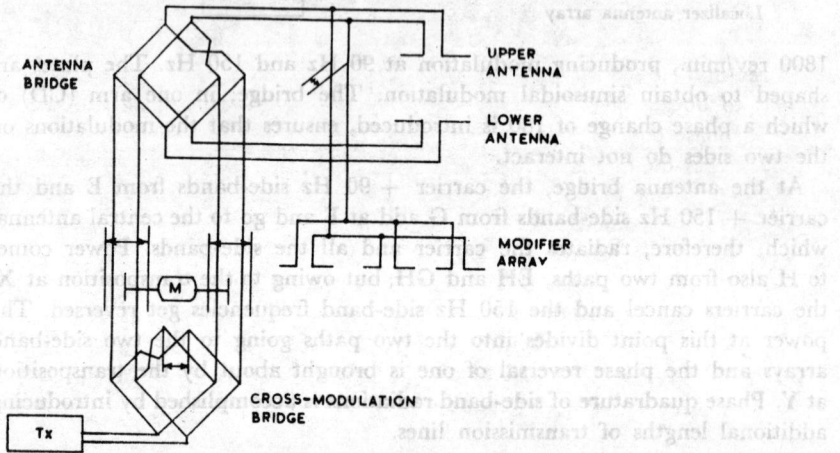

Fig. 6.6 Glide-slope antenna array

are similar to those of the localizer shown in Fig. 6.4. The carrier and side-bands are radiated by the lower antenna and the side-bands by the upper antenna, both of which are dipoles with a reflecting screen at the back. There is, in addition, the array called the modifier array, the function of which is explained in the following paragraph.

The glide-slope equipment and antenna have to be sited away from the runway so that they do not constitute a hazard. Generally the installation is sited 450 ft away from the centre line of the runway. The surfaces defined by equal differences in the depth of modulation (ddm) are hyperboloids of revolution with a vertical axis at the antenna.[20] The intersection of the equi-signal plane of the localizer and of this hyperboloid is another hyperbola which does not touch the runway. The preferred path of descent is, however, a straight line. At appreciable distances from the runway, the hyperbola approximates a straight line, but near the runway it tends to flatten out. To make the path nearly straight up to the touch-down point, a modifier antenna is some times used to correct for this, but the utility of this has been questioned and its use has generally been discontinued. The glide-slope antennas give several lobes of the type shown in Fig. 6.5 at higher elevations and it might appear that these might give rise to a number of false courses at higher angles. However, an examination of the modulation at each lobe shows that the first false course gives reversed indications, i.e. above the course, the 150 Hz modulation predominates and below the course the 90 Hz modulation predominates. Therefore, this cannot be mistaken for the correct course. The next false course, at three times the glide angle gives correct indications, but it is so steep that a pilot can easily make out that it is not the correct one.

(c) **Receiving Equipment**

The receiver is typically a crystal controlled multi-channel receiver. Separate receivers are required for the localiser and the glide-slope facilities, as they operate in widely different bands. One of the features of the receivers is a very efficient automatic gain control system. This keeps the output of the receiver constant when the input varies from 20 µV to 100,000 µV. To achieve a flat AGC characteristic over this range, the gain control is applied to the audio stages also. The efficient AGC ensures that the signal is held constant and in consequence, the meter indication depends only on the difference in modulation depths, i.e. upon the angular deviation from the course.

It is important, both in the localizer and the glide-slope, that the courses are maintained correctly and the modulation levels preserved. To ensure this, monitoring equipment is put up near the installation. These employ dipole antennas fixed at certain specified points on and off course, the signals from which are detected and processed to find the modulation components and monitor the course alignment, width and clearance. Departures from numerical values by more than certain specified amounts are made to operate alarm circuits.

The instrumentation part of the receiver is shown in Fig. 6.7(a). The output of the receiver is applied to two filters which separate the 90 Hz and 150 Hz signals, each of which is rectified by a bridge rectifier. The outputs of the rectifier are connected so as to give the difference between the rectified voltages and this is applied to the indicator coil. The balance control R_1 is used to compensate for different losses in the two rectifiers and filters. The resistors R_2, R_3 and the thermistor T are in the common branch which carries the total rectified current. The voltage across R_3 is applied to a coil which operates the

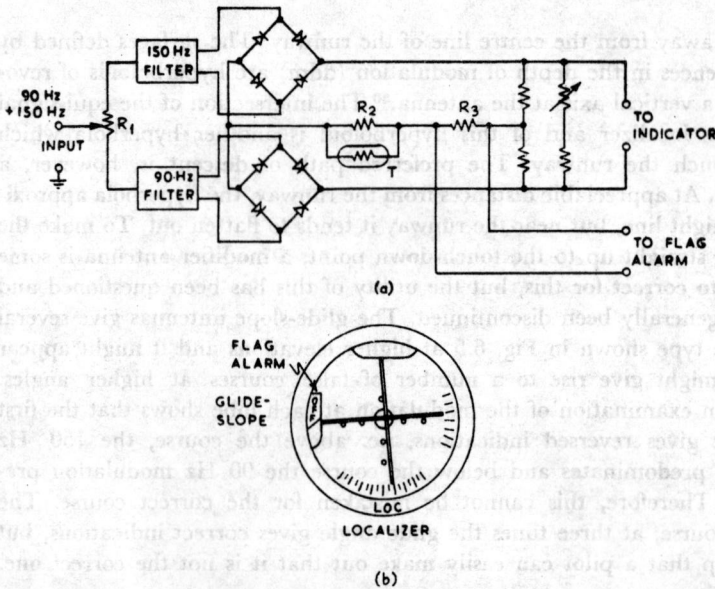

Fig. 6.7 Instrumentation part of ILS receiver [(a) Rectifier circuits feeding the indicator, (b) ILS indicator]

'flag alarm'. When the coil is not energized (because of the failure of the equipment or low signal, etc) it operates a flag which masks the pointer. If this were not there, an on-course indication would be read. The thermistor compensates for the changes in the resistance of the rectifier with temperature and prevents the temperature from affecting the apparent course width. Similar circuits are used in the instrumentation part of the localiser and glide-slope.

The indicator is shown in Fig. 6.7(b). It consists of a meter with two centre-zero movements. The horizontal needle indicates deviation from the glide-path and the vertical one, the deviation from the localizer. Each pointer gives a maximum deflection typically for a current of 150 μA.

(d) Course Sharpness and Width

The sharpness and width of the course are dependent on the relative depths of modulation of the 90 Hz and 150 Hz signals. The total signal modulation is defined by the relation: $M = (A + B)/C$, where M is the total signal modulation, A and B are the amplitudes of the 150 Hz and 90 Hz signals respectively and C is the carrier amplitude. The difference in the depth of modulation (ddm) of the two signals is given by $(A - B)/C$. A current proportional to this quantity drives the needle of a pointer, which, typically, has a full scale deflection of $+ 150 \mu A$. On-course, whether in the localizer or the glide-path, the ddm is zero. Off the course, one or the other of the modulations predominates and a deflection is obtained in the meter. In the localizer, full scale deflection corresponds to a ddm of 0·155, which occurs when the aircraft is 2° off the equi-signal course. In the glide-slope, a ddm of 0·175 is made to give a full scale deflection when the glide-angle deviates by a fifth of the slope angle (e.g $\pm$ 0·6° for 3° slope of the glide-path). In the neighbourhood of the null, the ddm is a linear function of the deviation from the equi-signal path.

The sharpness of the course, both in the localizer and glide-path is measured in terms of the ratio of the 90 Hz and 150 Hz side-band signals, the ratio being expressed in dB. This measure is called the 'clearance'. In the localizer, the clearance at $\pm$ 1·5° off the course is called 'course sharpness'.

(e) Site Effects in the ILS

The localizer and glide-slope courses are affected by the nature of the site on which they are installed. The operation of both these facilities being continuous wave, the presence of surface irregularities, hills, vegetation as well the nearby location of other aircraft affect the equi-signal course. So long as this does not introduce sharp bends, the course may still be 'flyable'. In difficult locations, it may be necessary to use special arrays which radiate as little energy as possible in directions other than those required. But as this may make it difficult for the aircraft to come within the beam, a subsidiary low-power transmission of the facility is made by the aid of which the aircraft can come into the beam of the more directive main transmitter. When it does so, the main beam takes over. The two transmissions differ in frequency by a small amount (a few kHz) and no retuning of the receiver is necessary. The stronger signal of the main beam takes over, i.e. the receiver responds to the stronger signal only. This phenomenon is called capture effect. The low power signal is called the 'clearance signal' and the high power one the 'directional signal'.

The polar diagram of a directional localizer ('capture effect localizer') is shown in Fig. 6.8. The clearance array acts as a low power localizer, using an

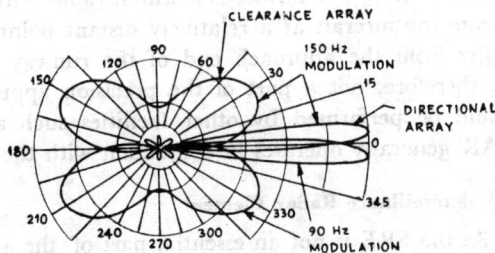

Fig. 6.8
Polar diagram of capture-effect localizer

eight loop array with a power output of 90 to 180 W at a frequency 4 kHz below the main localizer frequency. This pattern can be used at all azimuths and gives unambiguous information (i.e. whether to fly right or left). The directional array provides guidance within $\pm$ 10° of the centre line of the runway. The power radiated by this is low at other azimuth angles and any site irregularities in these directions will not cause course bends. At large azimuths, the clearance signal is stronger and the receiver locks on to it, and gives proper guidance.

(f) Marker Beacons

The ILS employs three marker beacons (Fig. 6.1) which give an indication in the aircraft when it passes over them. All of them operate at 75 MHz and work with an antenna which gives a fan-shaped beam which is typically $\pm 40°$ wide along the approach path and $\pm 80°$ perpendicular to it. The most distant one (from the end of the runway, called the outer marker (OM) is approximately 7 km from the touch down point on the runway. The radiation is modulated at 400 Hz, giving two dashes per sec. The second one, called the middle marker (MM) is placed where the glide path is 200 ft (approx. 60 m) which generally is about 1 km from the touch-down point. The modulation is at 1300 Hz with one dash every $\frac{2}{3}$ sec. The inner marker (which is not used at all airports) is placed where the glide-path is 100 ft (approx. 30m) above the ground. It is modulated at 3000 Hz, six dots per second. In the aircraft, a single receiver tuned to 75 MHz is employed. The output is available as an audio signal and also actuates three lamps, one for each marker beacon.

6.2 Ground-Controlled Approach System

This is a high-precision radar system sited near the airport runway, with the help of which a controller on the ground can bring the aircraft into approach zone and then guide it along the path of descent to a point very near the runway. The system consists of two separate radars, one called the surveillance radar element (SRE), and the other called the precision approach radar (PAR). The former is a search radar with a PPI display which helps to locate the aircraft at a relatively distant point and bring it to within a few miles from the approach end of the runway from the proper direction. It is, therefore, not a part of the precision approach system and its functions could be performed by other facilities such as airfield control radar. The PAR generally operates in conjuction with the ILS.

(a) Surveillance Radar Element

As the SRE is not an essential part of the approach system, it will not be dealt with here. The following data relating to an early version of SRE may however be noted.

Wavelength: 10 cm
Peak power: 80 kW
Pulse length: 0·5 μsec
Pulse repetition
    frequency: 2000 pulses/sec.

Scan rate: 30 rev/min.
Beam width in
      the horizontal plane: approx. 0·5°
The fan-shaped beam covers about 20° in the vertical plane.

(b) Precision Approach Radar

This precision radar has a maximum range of about 15-20 km and scans the approach zone both in azimuth and elevation. The precise performance and display details depend to some extent on the manufacturer of the equipment and the data given below pertain to some equipment developed by the Standard Telephones and Cables.[21]

The radar has to scan a 20° azimuth sector and a 7° elevation sector to meet the operational requirements. The accuracy demanded in respect of the determined azimuth and elevation angles requires a beam width in the scanning direction of 0·5°. Therefore, two separate antennas are used for azimuth and elevation scannings. The antenna coverage in the dimension not scanned could theoretically cover the whole of the unscanned sector but practical considerations (e.g. limited transmitter power) preclude this and coverage is limited to 4°. This means that the elevation scan should be capable of azimuthal movement of 16° and the azimuthal scan, an elevation movement of 3°. The latter is rarely required if the coveragee is kept between 1° and 5° as few aircraft are likely to come at a greater angle of descent. The coverage of the antennas is shown diagrammatically in Fig. 6.9(a) and the location of the PAR in respect of the runway is shown in Fig. 6.9(b).

Since the precision of the PAR depends upon the precise determination of the beam position, it is required that the true beam position must be known at every instant with an accuracy better than 5′ of arc.

The PAR uses a single radar transmitter which is connected alternately to the two antennas, i.e. the two scans are interlaced. The data pertaining to the equipment mentioned are as follows:

Transmitted power (peak) .. 50 kW
Frequency .. 9080 MHz
Pulse width .. 0·18 μsec
Pulse repetition frequency .. 3·825 kHz
Range discrimination .. 200 ft
Azimuth discrimination .. 0·6°
Elevation discrimination .. 0·6°

Rapid scanning of the antenna beam is required in the PAR as the information has to be rapidly renewed. The narrow beam requirements given above dictate a large antenna aperture and, therefore, a physically large antenna (13 ft × 1·625 ft in the above equipment). Scanning by movement of the whole antenna presents practical problems and a different method which does not require the movement of the antenna system is adopted. This method, employs an array of dipoles fed from and mounted on a wave-guide the width of which is varied. The array consists of 209 dipoles spaced 1·92 cm apart

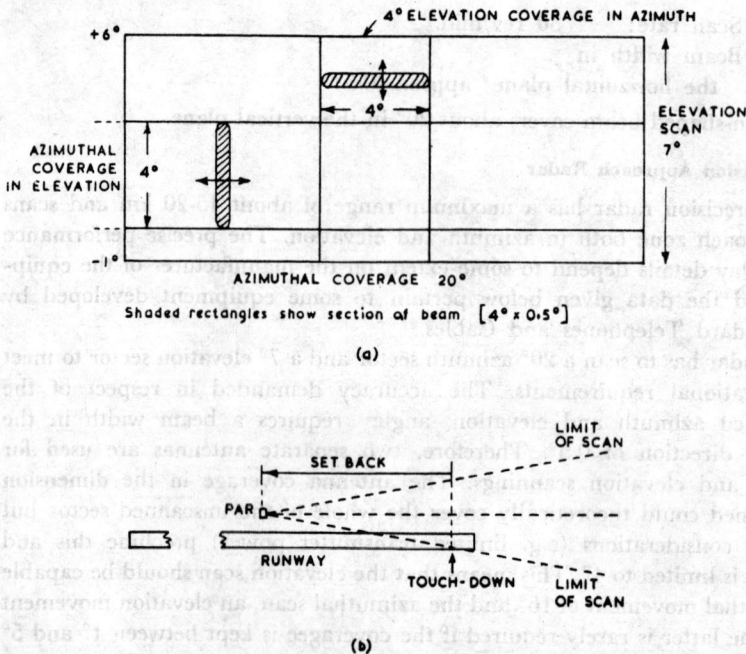

Fig. 6.9 [(a) Coverage of PAR antenna (b) and position of PAR with respect to the runway]

which are mounted on the side of the wave-guide and terminate in a probe which couples with the wave-guide and draws a certain calculated amount of power. Radio frequency power is fed at one end of the wave-guide and its far end is terminated with a resistance load so as to prevent reflections. The array produces a beam the width of which is nearly constant and the orientation of which is dependent on the wavelength in the guide. This wavelength can be altered by altering the width of the wave-guide. Fig. 6.10

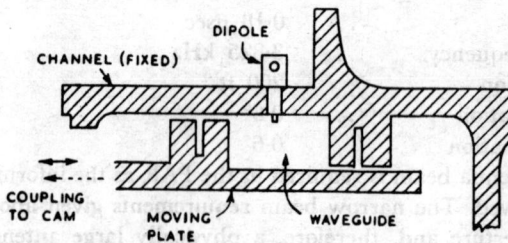

Fig. 6.10 "Squeezable" wave-guide

shows a section of the wave-guide indicating how the width of the wave-guide is altered. The change in the wavelength changes the relative phases of the current fed to the antennas and this has the effect of changing the direction of maximum radiation. The principle is similar to that employed in phase array radars for beam steering.[22] This wave-guide has been called a 'squeezable wave-guide'. Altering the section of the wave-guide presents a much simpler mechanical problem than the rotation of any array, because of the lightness of the parts involved.

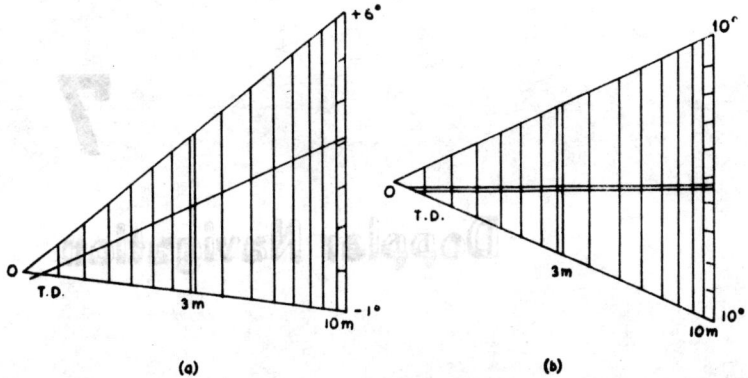

Fig. 6.11 PAR display [(a) elevation, (b) azimuth]. (Range shown in miles)

The data obtained by the PAR are displayed on two long-persistence cathode ray tubes, one displaying the range and elevation angle and the other the range and azimuth angle (Fig. 6.11). Note that the lines of constant range appear as straight lines instead of arcs of circles. Also, the angular sweeps appear expanded and the range sweep is progressively slowed down as the range increases. These deliberately introduced distortions help to increase the accuracy of angle measurements and also to increase range accuracy at the shorter ranges where it is most required. The distance markers appear at certain fixed ranges and angle markers at the ends of the display. The two display tubes are mounted on a single console and one controller uses both. The localizer and glide-slope courses may be permanently marked on the display so that the controller can know the position of the aircraft with respect to the desired path of descent.

While the radar itself is located near the runway end, the console may be in the control tower. The two points will be connected by cables which carry the control signals and video data.

Equipment of the type described is capable of resolving targets which are 60 m apart. The accuracy is such that at a distance of 1 mile, it is possible to detect deviations from glide-slope of as little as 8 m.

7

Doppler Navigation

A SELF-CONTAINED dead-reckoning navigation system requires some device within the craft for finding its velocity vector with respect to some reference direction (such as the true North) on the surface of the earth. The Doppler navigation system is 'self-contained' in this sense. It employs the Doppler effect to determine the velocity of the craft in a frame of coordinates fixed with respect to the aircraft. The velocity with respect to the conventional earth coordinates such as the true or magnetic North is obtained by combining this information with the direction of the aircraft which may be obtained from a gyrocompass. The complete Doppler navigation equipment generally includes a computer which automatically computes navigational data required, such as the track, the distance covered etc. by combining the velocity data obtained by Doppler effect with the directional reference provided by auxiliary means. Doppler navigation is used only in aircraft.

7.1 The Doppler Effect

The equipment used for Doppler navigation is a Doppler radar carried in the aircraft which directs a beam of electro-magnetic waves towards the earth. Some of the energy re-radiated by the earth towards the aircraft is received and comparison is made between the frequencies of the transmitted and received signals. When the aircraft has a component of velocity in the direction of the beam, the difference frequency (called the Doppler shift) is nearly proportional to the velocity component. This is Doppler effect, which holds good for all types of waves, though in this case we are concerned with electromagnetic waves.

Let the radar be moving with a velocity which has a component v_r in the direction of the beam (Fig. 7.1). Let f_t be the transmitted frequency. The

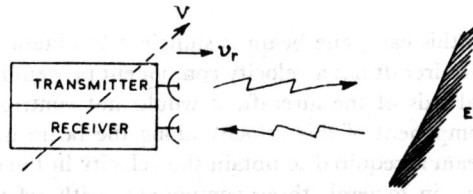

Fig. 7.1 Principle of Doppler radar

frequency, as measured at the stationary reflecting object (E) is $f_t \left(1 + \dfrac{v_r}{c}\right)$ where c is the velocity of electromagnetic waves. The reflected waves have this frequency but when they are received by the radar, because of the motion of the receiver towards the object, the received frequency is increased in the ratio $\left(1 + \dfrac{v_r}{c}\right)$. The received frequency f_r is, therefore, given by:

$$f_r = f_t \left(1 + \frac{v_r}{c}\right)^2 = f_t \left(1 + \frac{2v_r}{c} + \frac{v_r^2}{c^2}\right) \qquad 7.1$$

The term $\dfrac{v_r^2}{c^2}$ is almost always negligible because of the high value of c. So the 'Doppler shift' f_D may be taken to be:

$$f_D = f_r - f_t \approx f_t \frac{2v_r}{c} = \frac{2v_r}{\lambda} \qquad 7.2$$

where λ is the wavelength of the transmitted signal. By mixing the received signal with a part of the transmitted signal, f_D may be obtained and v_r determined from Eq. 7.2. Note that f_D may be either positive or negative, depending on the sign of v_r. If the radar is moving towards the object (Fig. 7.1), the received frequency is higher, and the Doppler shift is positive. If it is moving away from the object, the received frequency is lower and the Doppler shift is negative.

7.2 Beam Configurations

Consider an aircraft flying over the earth, transmitting electromagnetic waves in a narrow beam making an angle ϕ with the horizontal (Fig. 7.2). If

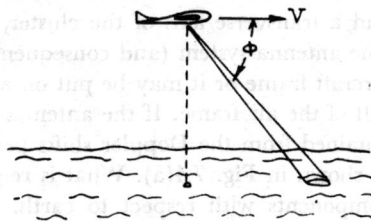

Fig. 7.2
Doppler radar in an aircraft in level flight

the aircraft is in level flight, and the beam is directed in the vertical plane containing the forward velocity V of the aircraft, the component of the velocity in the direction of the beam is $V\cos\phi$ and the Doppler shift is $\dfrac{2V\cos\phi}{\lambda}$.

In this case, one beam is sufficient to obtain V, as ϕ is a known angle. But if the aircraft has a velocity component perpendicular to this, i.e. to the longitudinal axis of the aircraft, it would not contribute to the Doppler shift, as the component of this velocity along the beam is zero. Therefore, more than one beam is required to obtain the velocity in the general case. The aircaft velocity has, in general, three components with reference to a system of orthogonal coordinates fixed with reference to the aircraft frame. These are the forward (or heading) velocity along its longitudinal axis, the drift velocity perpendicular to it and the vertical velocity. In general, therefore, three beams are necessary to obtain the three components. In some cases, four beams are used. Some of the configurations used in Doppler radar are shown in Fig. 7.3 in plan.

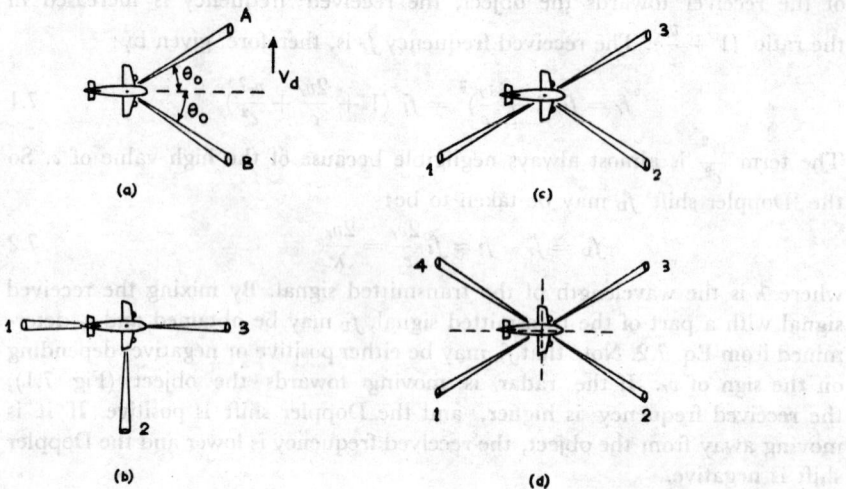

Fig. 7.3 Doppler radar beam configurations [(a) two-beam non-Janus system, (b) three-beam Janus-T, (c) three-beam Janus-λ, (d) four-beam Janus (Janus-X)]

In all cases, the position of the set of beams, called the 'beam cluster' has a fixed relation to the antenna system, and we may define a longitudinal axis and a transverse axis of the cluster, as shown by dotted lines in Fig. 7.3(d). The antenna system (and consequently the beam cluster) may be fixed to the aircraft frame or it may be put on a stabilized mount corrected for pitch and roll of the air frame. If the antenna is not stabilized, the velocity components obtained from the Doppler shifts pertain to the aircraft reference coordinates as shown in Fig. 7.4(a). What is required for navigation is the set of velocity components with respect to earth. With a stabilized antenna [Fig. 7.4(b)] this is directly obtained. If a fixed antenna system is employed, the velocity components measured have to be converted to the earth system of coordinates by taking into account the pitch and roll angles.[20] The effect of pitch and roll is discussed qualitatively for some of the beam configurations in the next paragraph.

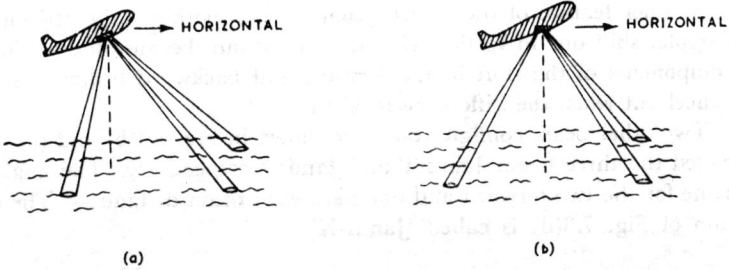

Fig. 7.4 Antenna system (a) fixed to the aircraft (b) and stabilized for pitch and roll

Fig. 7.3(a) shows a two-beam system, in which the beams, (marked A and B) when projected to a horizontal plane make an angle θ_0 with the longitudinal axis of the antenna. (This will coincide with the heading direction, unless the antenna is turned). When there is no drift, the Doppler shifts obtained with the two beams are equal. When there is a drift in the direction indicated in the figure, the Doppler shift of A increases and that of B decreases, both in proportion to the drift velocity. By taking the sum of the two frequencies, the heading velocity is obtained, and by taking the difference, the drift velocity is obtained. A vertical component of the velocity, by itself, changes both the Doppler frequencies equally and this may be wrongly interpreted as a forward (or backward) velocity depending on the sign of the change. So this beam configuration is subject to errors unless the vertical velocity information is obtained by other means and used to correct the shift. Another disadvantage of this antenna system is that it is sensitive to the vertical attitude of the aircraft. Pitching, for example, results in the change of the angles γ of Fig. 7.5 and the corresponding change introduces errors. To overcome this, the antenna system has to be stabilized for pitch to a high degree of accuracy.

On the other hand, the Janus system* of Fig. 7.3(d) is relatively insensitive to pitch and roll of the aircraft as the following qualitative reasoning will show. With this Janus system, the Doppler shift of the rear beam is subtracted from that of the front beam. (It is to be noted that the former is negative and the latter is positive and, therefore, the magnitudes of the shifts are added). In level flight, the two shifts are equal. When there is a pitch angle making the front of the aircraft lower than its rear, the front beam depression angle increases and the back beam depression angle decreases. This tends to decrease the magnitude of the Doppler shift of the front beam and increase the magnitude of the shift of the rear beam. So the sum of the magnitudes tends to remain constant. For small angles of pitch, the changes are nearly equal and nearly complete compensation results. This system is, therefore, less sensitive to pitch than the 'non-Janus' system. The antenna system, though requiring stabilization, does not require such a high degree of stabilization as the 'non-Janus' system.

* Janus is the name of a Greek god who could look both ways. The name is used as the antenna looks both forward and backward. In contrast, the arrangement in Fig. 7.3(a) is called 'non-Janus'.

Another feature of the Janus system is that, with a stabilized antenna, the Doppler shift due to vertical velocity cancels out, because the vertical velocity components of the shift in the forward and backward beams are equal and cancel out when the difference is taken.

Two other beam configurations are shown in Fig. 7.3(b) and (c). These are called the three beam Janus-T and Janus-λ respectively. The angle θ_0 is the same for the two forward and one backward beam of Janus-λ. The configuration of Fig. 7.3(d) is called 'Janus-X'.

7.3 Doppler Frequency Equations

The Doppler shifts obtained with each of the four beams of the Janus-X antenna will now be calculated. For simplicity we will assume that the antenna is stabilized for pitch and roll. In the case of fixed antennas also similar equations can be obtained but the velocities computed will have to be converted to those in earth coordinates by taking into account the pitch and roll angles, as stated earlier.

The Doppler shift obtained with any beam is obtained by taking the component of the aircraft velocity vector in the direction of the beam. This is done by taking the component of each of three orthogonal components of the aircraft velocity in the direction of the beam and summing them. As we are assuming that the antenna system is stabilized, the three components are the vertical component V_V and two horizontal components V_H and V_D, the former being in the vertical plane containing the longitudinal axis of the aircraft and the latter being perpendicular to this. Fig. 7.5(a) shows one of the

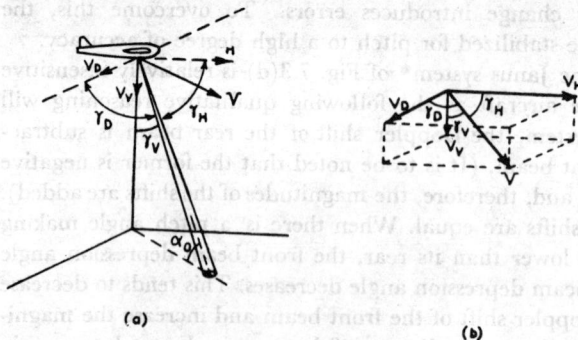

Fig. 7.5 Geometry of one beam of a Janus-X Doppler radar
[(a) beam orientation, (b) velocity vectors]

beams positioned in this frame of coordinates (the earth coordinates) and Fig. 7.5(b) shows the three velocity vectors. The velocity components for the four beams of the James-X in Fig. 7.4 are as given in Eqn. 7.3 to 7.6.*

* Any three of these equations are sufficient to solve for V_H, V_D and V_V. But when all the four beams are present, as in Janus X, the solutions take a form which is simple to implement.

$$v_1 = - V_H \cos \gamma_H + V_D \cos \gamma_D + V_V \cos \gamma_V \qquad 7.3$$
$$v_2 = V_H \cos \gamma_H + V_D \cos \gamma_D + V_V \cos \gamma_V \qquad 7.4$$
$$v_3 = V_H \cos \gamma_H - V_D \cos \gamma_D + V_V \cos \gamma_V \qquad 7.5$$
$$v_4 = V_H \cos \gamma_H - V_D \cos \gamma_D + V_V \cos \gamma_V \qquad 7.6$$

Here γ_H, γ_D and γ_V are the angles between the velocity components V_H, V_D and V_V and the beam, as shown in Fig. 7.5(b). Perfect symmetry of the four beams is assumed. The direction cosines are given by:

$$\cos \gamma_H = \cos \alpha_0 \cos \theta_0; \quad \cos \gamma_D = \cos \alpha_0 \sin \theta_0; \quad \cos \gamma_V = \sin \alpha_0 \qquad 7.7$$

Here, α_0 is the depression angle of the beam, i.e. the angle between the beam and the plane of the antenna. All angles relating to a beam are with the 'beam centroid' as reference. The centroid will be defined later.

The relative velocity components (v_1, v_2, v_3, v_4) are obtained by multiplying the corresponding Doppler shifts $f_{D_1}, f_{D_2}, f_{D_3}$ and f_{D_4} assumed to be available individually, by the factor $\lambda/2$. The solution of simultaneous Eqs. 7.3 to 7.6 gives the velocity components V_H, V_D and V_V. For the Janus-X arrangement, the solutions are readily obtained by inspection:

$$V_H = \frac{v_2 + v_3 - (v_1 + v_4)}{4 \cos \gamma_H} = \frac{\lambda}{8} \frac{(f_{D2} + f_{D3}) - (f_{D1} + f_{D4})}{\cos \alpha_0 \sin \theta_0} \qquad 7.8$$

$$V_D = \frac{(v_1 + v_2) - (v_3 + v_4)}{4 \cos \gamma_D} = \frac{\lambda}{8} \frac{(f_{D1} + f_{D2}) - (f_{D3} + f_{D4})}{\cos \alpha_0 \sin \theta_0} \qquad 7.9$$

$$V_V = \frac{v_1 + v_2 + v_3 + v_4}{4 \cos \gamma_D} = \frac{\lambda}{8} \frac{(f_{D1} + f_{D2} + f_{D3} + f_{D4})}{\sin \alpha_0} \qquad 7.10$$

Similar solutions may be obtained for the 3-beam Janus-λ antenna system, by using only Eqs. 7.3, 7.4 and 7.5. Actually, in Janus-X system, only $(f_{D3} - f_{D1})$ and $(f_{D2} - f_{D4})$ may be available due to the nature of implementation of the Doppler shift measurement. In this case, only V_H and V_D can be found and V_V cannot be determined.

An important parameter of a Doppler radar is the angle between the longitudinal axis of the antenna and the beam centroid, i.e. the angle γ_H in the Janus systems. The smaller is this angle, larger is the Doppler shift for a given velocity. But, for small values of γ_H, the signal returned from water surface becomes very small. This puts a lower limit to the value of this angle. A compromise is effected between the requirements of high sensitivity and appreciable return from the surface of water. The angle has generally a value between 65° and 80°. The value of the angle θ_0 is governed by sensitivity to drift velocity. Larger values of θ_0 give greater sensitivity to drift.

7.4 Track Stabilization

Eqs. 7.8 to 7.10 pertain to an antenna system in which the principal axis of the antenna system is in the same vertical plane as the aircraft longitudinal axis or heading. Such an antenna system is said to be *heading-stabilized*. In this case, the two horizontal components of the velocity, V_H and V_D are separately computed and the actual direction of motion of the aircraft (the 'track'), can be computed. The angle between the heading and track is called *drift-angle* (δ) and is given by the relation:

$$\tan \delta = \frac{V_D}{V_H} \text{ or } \delta = \text{arc tan} \frac{V_D}{V_H} \qquad 7.11$$

and the track speed $V_g = (V_H^2 + V_D^2)^{1/2} = V_H \sec \delta$.

There is an alternative type of mechanization, in which the antenna system is rotated about the vertical axis by a servo-system which is actuated by the drift component V_D. The antenna system is turned until the drift component reduces to zero. The track speed is given in this case by V_H itself. The axis of the antenna is then oriented in the direction of the track. This type of antenna is called *track-stabilized* or *drift-angle stabilized* antenna. The orientation of the beam cluster, when there is a drift, is illustrated for the two types of antennas in Fig. 7.6.

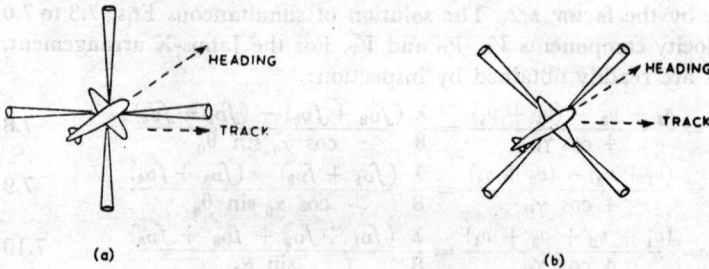

Fig. 7.6 Beam configuration [(a) antenna heading-stabilized, (b) antenna track-stabilized]

7.5 Doppler Spectrum

The Doppler shift in the above analysis has been taken as the frequency corresponding to the 'beam centroid'. If the beams were very narrow, essentially a single Doppler shift frequency would be obtained. But the antenna beams have finite width (generally about 4°) and cover a number of values of depression angle. The returns are consequently of different frequencies from different parts of the beam, and the resultant shift has the nature of a narrow-band frequency spectrum. The various scattering elements in the area illuminated by the beam give returns at different frequencies and in random phase. The spectrum, therefore, resembles that of narrow-band noise, superposed on white Gaussian noise which is always present. Fig. 7.7 depicts the type of spectrum obtained with Doppler radar. The two small peaks on either side of the main peak are caused by side lobes in the antenna pattern and do not interfere with the frequency measurements. The shape of the main spectrum is approximately Gaussian. The amplitude of the peak is a function of radar parameters (transmitted power, antenna aperture, range, etc.) and the back-scattering property of the terrain. The Doppler frequency which has been referred to so far is the mean of this spectral distribution. The corresponding angle defines the 'beam centroid'.

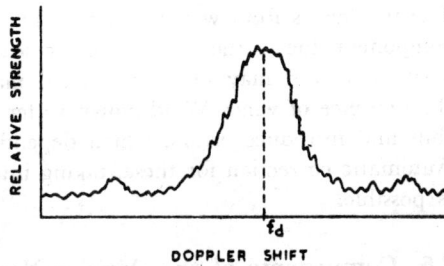

Fig. 7.7
The Doppler spectrum

The Doppler radar return, to a first approximation, has maximum strength in the direction of beam and falls off on either side in proportion to the two-way gain of the antenna. The approximation is due to the assumption that the beam scattering properties of the terrain are uniform over the area illuminated by the beam and that the effect of the inverse-square-law on the strength of the return is not appreciable, i.e. the nearest and farthest points on the ground illuminated by the beam are nearly at the same distance. With this assumption, we can calculate the half-power band-width of the Doppler signal. The Doppler shift is given by:

$$f_D = \frac{2V \cos\gamma}{\lambda}$$

If the beam width is $\Delta\gamma$ between the half-power points, the upper and lower half-power points giving Doppler shifts f_{D1} and f_{D2} differ by Δf_D, given by:

$$f_{D1} - f_{D2} = \frac{2V}{\lambda}\left[\cos\left(\gamma - \frac{\Delta\gamma}{2}\right) - \cos\left(\gamma + \frac{\Delta\gamma}{2}\right)\right]$$

$$\Delta f_D \approx \frac{2V}{\lambda} \cdot \sin\gamma \, \Delta\gamma$$

The width of this spectrum is proportional to the central Doppler frequency. The relative width of the spectrum, $\Delta f_D/f_D$ is given by:

$$\frac{\Delta f_D}{f_D} = \frac{\sin\gamma \; \Delta\gamma}{\cos\gamma} = \tan\gamma \; \Delta\gamma \qquad\qquad 7.12$$

This quantity is generally between 15% and 25%.

The assumption of uniform back-scattering properties of the terrain holds good over land but is not valid over still water, where the back-scatter changes with the value of γ, being higher for the higher values of γ and decreasing as γ decreases. This tends to distort the spectrum of the return, which will no longer be symmetrical but tends to have a peak on the lower side of the frequency corresponding to the beam centroid. This could cause errors (called 'over-water calibration shift' errors) in the computed velocity. In the simpler Doppler navigation equipment, the error is corrected to a fair approximation by changing the calibration by a switch (equivalent to a change of γ). More sophisticated techniques, such as lobe-switching are employed in modern versions of the equipment.[20]

There are other sources of errors associated with navigation over water.

The first arises from water currents. The measured velocities then include a component due to the velocity of the scattering surface. These are generally very small and may be compensated manually. The second type arises in the presence of wind. Wind-blown water particles contribute to the Doppler shift and introduce errors, which depend on the wind direction and speed. Automatic correction for these, taking into account the surface wind velocity is possible.

7.6 Components of the Doppler Navigation System

The various components which go to make up the complete Doppler navigation system are shown in Fig. 7.8. The functions of the various blocks are as

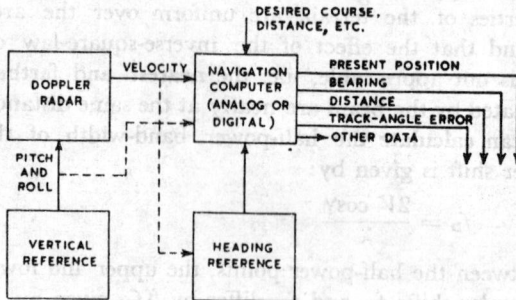

Fig. 7.8 The Doppler navigation system

follows: the *Doppler radar* gives the velocity components of the aircraft. If the antenna is stabilized, the pitch and roll information obtained from the *vertical reference* is utilized in the radar itself. If the antenna is not stabilized, the pitch and roll information is used by the computer to compute the velocity in earth coordinates. The *heading reference* is fed to the computer to compute the track information in respect of the desired coordinate system on earth. In the case of the track-stabilized antenna, the drift-angle output may be combined with the heading before being fed to the computer. The *navigational computer* which may be of the analog or the digital type, computes from the input information in respect of velocity vector, the necessary navigational information. The desired course and distance to be travelled may also be given as inputs to the computer and the distance to be covered, present position, track-angle error and other data for use in navigation may be obtained as outputs of the computer and suitably displayed.

In the following sections, a brief account of the principal part of the system, viz. the Doppler radar, is given.

7.6.1 Doppler Radar Equipment

The Doppler radar equipment consists of a transmitter, a receiver, an antenna system and a 'frequency-tracker'. The functions of the first three components are self-evident. The function of the frequency-tracker is to locate the centre frequency of the Doppler spectrum and give a sinusoidal output at that frequency. The transmitter operates in one of the two microwave bands— the X-band or the K-band, in the region of 9 GHz or 13 GHz respectively. The Doppler radar may be either of the pulsed type or the continuous wave type.

In pulsed radars, the Doppler frequency is obtained by heterodyning the received pulses with either a continuous wave or a pulse from another beam. The output thus obtained consists of samples of the Doppler wave-form, each sample being of the duration of the pulse and the sampling rate being the pulse recurrence frequency. To reconstruct the wave-form, the number of samples per second (i.e. the pulse recurrence frequency (prf)) must be higher than twice the highest frequency in the wave-form. This is a consequence of the sampling theorem. For supersonic aircraft, with the radar frequency in the 10-13 GHz region, the highest Doppler frequency may be a few tens of kHz. This dictates the use of a prf of the order of 100 kHz, in contrast to search radars where the prf may be of the order of a few hundred Hz. As a result of the high prf, the Doppler shift can be measured unambiguously while the range cannot be determined unambiguously.

Pulsed Doppler radar may be one of the two types—the incoherent (or self-coherent)-type and the coherent-type. In the incoherent operation, the phase of the radiation will, in general, change from pulse to pulse. In order to obtain the Doppler shift, the pulses received from two opposite beams, which arrive at the same time, are compared. In the four-beam Janus system, this would be accomplished by first pulsing the beams 1 and 3 and then the beams 2 and 4. The two Doppler shifts $(f_{D1} - f_{D3})$ and $(f_{D2} - f_{D4})$ so obtained are then processed for velocity information. With this arrangement, it is not possible to obtain the vertical velocity or the sense of the velocity (forward or backward). Another requirement of the incoherent Janus-X system is that the returns of the forward and backward beams must overlap, which implies that the range associated with the beams must be the same. This condition is satisfied when the antenna is stabilized and when the aircraft is in level flight. To facilitate this overlap, a special type of antenna beam is sometimes employed (Fig. 7.9.) This beam has the property that over its wider dimension, the

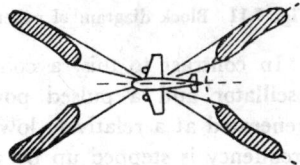

Fig. 7.9
Shaping of beam to facilitate pulse overlap

angle γ is constant, thereby ensuring that the Doppler shift associated with the various parts of the beam has the same value. But because of the spread in the area of ground illuminated, the pulse returns are wider in time and overlap is facilitated.

The block diagram of an incoherent system is shown in Fig. 7.10. A pulsed magnetron is used as the transmitter and this is switched to the beam pairs (1-3, 2-4) sequentially. A duplexer is used to permit common transmit-receive antenna operation. The received signal is applied to a super-heterodyne receiver, the output of which is the Doppler frequency signal. Automatic frequency control (AFC) of the local oscillator is necessary at these frequencies and, therefore, a sample of the transmitted signal is taken from a directional coupler and applied to the AFC circuit.

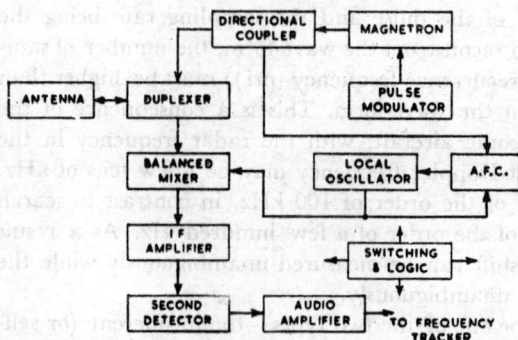

Fig. 7.10 Block diagram of the incoherent pulsed Doppler system

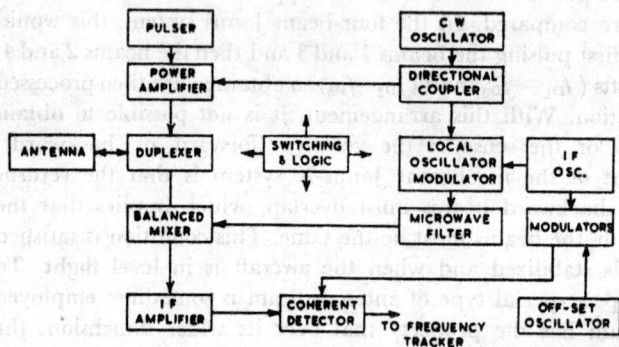

Fig. 7.11 Block diagram of coherent pulsed Doppler system

In contrast to this, a coherent Doppler radar employs a continuous wave oscillator and a pulsed power-amplifier (Fig. 7.11). The oscillations are generated at a relatively low frequency by a quartz-crystal oscillator and the frequency is stepped up by a chain of multipliers using step-recovery diodes or varactors. The local oscillator frequency is generated by heterodyning the oscillations at the transmission frequency with an oscillator at the intermediate frequency. The output of the mixer is, therefore, centred at the intermediate frequency (IF). The mixer and IF amplifier are followed by a coherent detector to which the other input is a reference frequency voltage. This reference frequency is obtained by mixing the IF with an 'off-set' oscillator output and taking the difference frequency output. By appropriately setting the off-set oscillator, both negative and positive Doppler shifts are obtainable. The coherent Doppler system is inherently capable of detecting the sense of the velocity as well as the vertical velocity, which is not possible with the incoherent system. The disadvantage of the coherent pulsed system is its greater complexity.

Pulse Doppler systems have a high pulse recurrence frequency as mentioned earlier and a relatively high duty ratio. At certain altitudes (which depend on the prf), the ground return for one pulse arrives at or near the time of transmission of the next pulse or some other succeeding pulse and is, therefore, gated out partially or fully. This phenomenon is called 'altitude hole' and may produce at low altitudes serious errors due to signal elimination and spectral weighting.[20] Altitude holes may be eliminated by changing or 'wobbling' the prf or by making the repetition frequency depend on the range in such a manner that the returns do not arrive at the time of transmission of a pulse.

7.6.2 Continuous Wave Doppler Radar

Continuous waves may also be used in Doppler radar. In this case, separate transmitting and receiving antennas are required for preventing the transmitter output from entering the receiver. The antennas also generally have to be separated physically. Except for this, the equipment is simpler, as the pulsing of the transmitter is avoided and a reference signal (part of the transmitter output) is always available (Fig. 7.12). The block diagram shows the

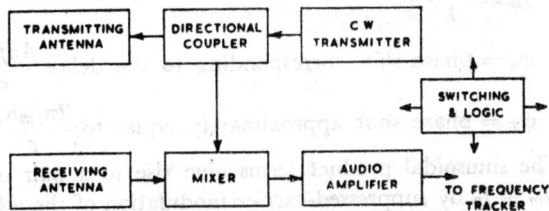

Fig. 7.12 Block diagram of continuous wave Doppler radar

essential parts of the system.The Doppler difference frequency is obtained by direct heterodyning of the transmitted and received signals. This is equivalent to having an intermediate frequency of zero, and is called *homodyne* reception. The difference signal is amplified in an audio amplifier and applied to the frequency tracker. It is to be noted that homodyne operation does not permit the sense of the velocity to be indicated.

The continuous wave Doppler radar is subject to spurious effects introduced by reflection from nearby objects, turbulent air, precipitation, etc.

Generally, fixed antenna systems are used with this type of Doppler radar. The direct leakage of signal from the transmitter to the receiver limits the maximum power that can be employed and hence satisfactory operation is limited to lower attitudes.

7.6.3 Frequency-Modulated Continuous-Wave Doppler Radar

Some of the disadvantages of the CW Doppler radar are overcome by the use of frequency modulation. In this system, the transmission is frequency modulated and the Doppler shift of one of the higher order side-band terms is measured. Consider a transmitted waveform of the type

$$\sin\left(2\pi f_0 t + \frac{\Delta f}{f_m} \sin 2\pi f_m t\right)$$

where f_0 is the carrier frequency; f_m the modulating frequency; and Δf, half the frequency excursion (maximum minus the minimum frequency).

This wave is returned, after a delay, with a change f_D in its frequency. It can be shown[22] that the signals containing the difference frequency f_D are of the form:

$$
\begin{aligned}
v_0 = {}& \mathcal{J}_0(D)\cos(2\pi f_D t - \phi_0) + 2\mathcal{J}_1(D)\sin(2\pi f_D t - \phi_0)\cos(2\pi f_m t - \phi_m) \\
& - 2\mathcal{J}_2(D)\cos(2\pi f_D t - \phi_0)\cos2(2\pi f_m t - \phi_m) \\
& - 2\mathcal{J}_3(D)\sin(2\pi f_D t - \phi_0)\cos3(2\pi f_m t - \phi_m)
\end{aligned}
\tag{7.13}
$$

where $\mathcal{J}_0, \mathcal{J}_1, \mathcal{J}_2$, etc. are Bessel functions of the first kind and order 0,1,2, etc.

$D = \dfrac{\Delta f}{f_m}\sin 2\pi f_m \dfrac{R_0}{c}$

$R_0 =$ distance to the target at time $t = 0$

$c =$ velocity of propagation

$V_r =$ the velocity component along the beam

$f_D = \dfrac{2V_r}{\lambda}$

$\phi_0 =$ phase shift corresponding to the delay $\dfrac{4\pi f_0 R_0}{c}$

$\phi_m =$ phase shift approximately equal to $\dfrac{2\pi f_m R_0}{c}$

The sinusoidal product terms give rise to a pair of frequencies of the type $nf_m \pm f_D$ by suppressed-carrier modulation of the nth order Bessel term nf_m by the Doppler shift f_D. The spectrum would appear as shown in Fig. 7.13. The

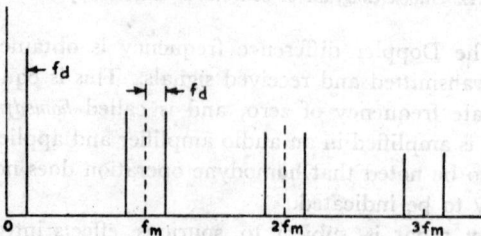

Fig. 7.13 Frequency spectrum of frequency modulated Doppler radar

technique described above (i.e. taking the difference between the transmitted and received frequencies) is equivalent to homodyne reception and information regarding the sense of the velocity is lost. The Doppler frequency may be extracted from any of the side-bands by heterodyning with the corresponding harmonic of the modulating frequency. The amplitude of the Doppler signal depends on both the order of the Bessel side-band and the value of D. Bessel functions of the first kind and orders zero to 3 are shown in Fig. 7.14, as a

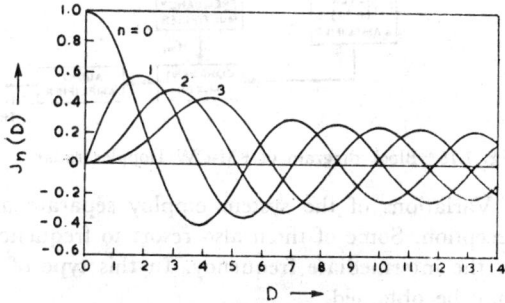

Fig. 7.14 Bessel functions of orders 0 to 3

function of D. The advantage of employing frequency modulation and choosing one of the higher order Bessel sidebands is evident from this. When the order of the Bessel sideband is 2 or higher, the corresponding amplitude of $\mathcal{J}_n(D)$ is very low for low values of D. Since D is proportional to $\sin 2\pi f_m \dfrac{R_0}{c}$, this implies that direct feed from transmitter and returns from objects very near (low R_0) will give very low outputs and the disadvantage of CW Doppler is eliminated. However, this also implies that low altitude performance may not be satisfactory. In addition, FM-CW technique has the drawback of 'altitude holes' in common with the pulsed system. The presence of altitude holes arises from the fact that when $2\pi f_m \dfrac{R_0}{c}$ is a multiple of π, say $m\pi$, D becomes zero. Since $R_0 = h \operatorname{cosec} \psi$ where ψ is the depression angle, at certain altitudes given by $mc/(2 f_m \operatorname{cosec} \psi)$, the signals become zero. This disadvantage is overcome by either making f_m so low that even at the maximum useable altitude, the hole is not reached or by making f_m very high and wobbling the modulation frequency.

A block diagram of FM-CW Doppler radar is shown in Fig. 7.15. This shows a system using a common antenna for transmission and reception and homodyne reception. The received signal is mixed with sample of the transmitted signal in a balanced mixer and the desired side band is filtered and applied to a coherent mixer. The output of the filter will have frequencies $nf_m \pm f_D$. This is mixed with the nth harmonic of the FM oscillator in the coherent mixer, the output of which will then be at the frequency f_D. After amplification, the signal is fed to the frequency tracker.

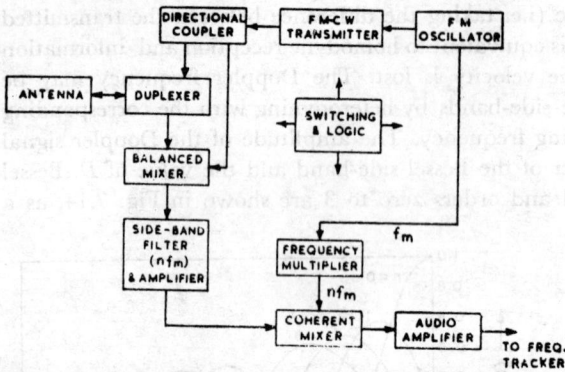

Fig. 7.15 Block diagram of FM-CW Doppler radar

Variations of the system employ separate antennas for transmission and reception. Some of them also resort to frequency changing and amplification at the intermediate frequency. In this type of equipment, sense information may be obtained.

7.6.4 Frequency Trackers

The frequency tracker locates the centre of the noise-like Doppler spectrum and gives as output the pure signal of this frequency. There are various configurations of the frequency tracker but most of them employ a tracking oscillator, the frequency of which is compared with the spectrum in a discriminator-type device and the error signal generated when the oscillator deviates from the centre of the spectrum is fed back to correct the frequency of the oscillator. One configuration (called the 'two-filter' tracker) is shown in Fig. 7.16. In this arrangement, actually a single filter is used but the oscillator

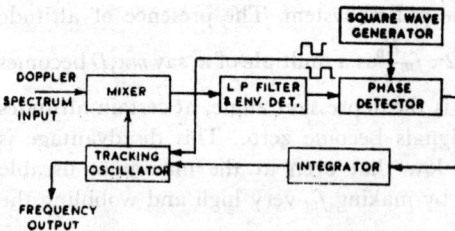

Fig. 7.16 Block diagram of a two-filter frequency tracker

frequency is switched by a square wave and takes on alternately two values which are separated by the spectrum width. The oscillator output is mixed with the Doppler signal and then passed through a low-pass filter and envelope detector. The output of the filter is a square wave which is applied to the phase detector, the other input to which is the output of the square wave oscillator. The phase of the first input in relation to the second (i.e. in-phase or 180° out of phase) determines the sign of the output of the phase detector, which serves as the error signal. This is integrated and applied to the voltage-controlled oscillator to change its mean frequency. The zero-error condition is obtained when the two frequencies of the oscillator straddle the centre frequency of the Doppler spectrum. For details of implementation of this arrangement, see Ref. 20. Though many different configurations of the frequency tracker are in vogue, their performances are all nearly the same in respect of complexity, operation under low signal/noise ratio conditions, etc.

7.7 Doppler Range Equation

The magnitude of the signal received from the ground by the Doppler radar is an important parameter as it determines the maximum range at which the equipment operates. The signal strength received may be obtained from the radar range equation suitably modified to the situation pertaining in Doppler radar. In its simplest form, the radar range equation is given by [Ref. 23 Eq. 26-3]:

$$P_r = \frac{P_T \, G_T \, S \, A_e}{(4\pi R^2)^2}$$

where
P_r = received signal power
P_T = power of the transmitted signal
　　　(the peak power in pulsed radar systems)
G_T = gain of the transmitting antenna
S = radar cross-section of the target
A_e = effective area of the receiving antenna and
R = distance of the target.

This equation will now be applied to Doppler radar. In Doppler radar, the target is the ground itself and its radar cross-section is related to the area of the ground illuminated by the beam. Such a target is called a 'beam-filling' target. Let the solid angle of the beam be w steradians and the angle of incidence of the beam at the ground be ψ (Fig. 7.17). The area of the ground illuminated by the beam is then $\dfrac{R^2 w}{\cos\psi}$. The scattering cross-section of the

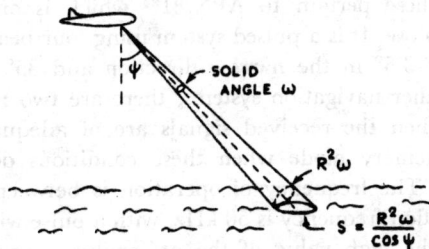

Fig. 7.17 Target area in Doppler radar

target is proportional to this area. If we denote by σ_0 the scattering cross-section per unit area illuminated, the factor S in the range Eq. 7.14 is replaced by $\dfrac{\sigma_0 R^2 w}{\cos\psi}$. The effective area of the antenna A_e is related to the antenna gain by the relation

$$G = \frac{4\pi A_e}{\lambda^2}$$

where λ is the wavelength of the radiation. Noting that the gain of an antenna is related to the solid angle of the beam by the relation [Ref. 22 Eq. 7.4] $G = \dfrac{4\pi}{w}$ the effective area reduces to $A_e = \dfrac{\lambda^2}{w}$. Substituting these in the range equation,

$$P_r = \frac{P_T G_T}{16\pi^2 R^4} \cdot \frac{\sigma_0 w R^2}{\cos\psi}\frac{\lambda^2}{w}$$

$$= \frac{P_T G_T \lambda^2 \sigma_0}{16\pi^2 R^2 \cos\psi} \qquad 7.15$$

The signal/noise ratio at the IF [(s/n)/if] is obtained by dividing the received signal power by the available noise power $kT_0 B_{IF} F$ where B_{IF} is the IF bandwidth, F is the noise figure of the receiver, k the Boltzmann constant and T_0 the standard temperature of 290°K. Substituting

$$(s/n)_{IF} = \frac{P_T G_T \lambda^2 \sigma_0}{16\pi^2 R^2 \; kT_0 B_{IF} F \; \cos\psi} \qquad 7.16$$

This equation could be further modified by including a factor which takes into account the non-uniform illumination of the scattering surface by the antenna beam pattern, the attenuation along the path of the beam, etc.[20]. However, the basic factors are evident from the above equation. In particular, it may be noted that the s/n ratio varies inversely as the square of the range and it is directly proportional to σ_0 which characterizes the nature of the scattering surface. While Eq. 7.16 gives the s/n ratio at IF, the factor of importance is the s/n ratio in the Doppler frequency band, which in general is different. A further factor is, therefore, necessary which takes into account the loss in the detector, and in FM-CW systems and the power in the particular band employed.

The parameters of a particular Doppler navigation system are given below. These pertain to APN/81[24] which is one of the early systems to be put to use. It is a pulsed system using four beam Janus antenna, with beam widths of 3·5° in the narrow direction and 35° in the wide direction. As in many other navigation systems, there are two modes of operation—a normal mode when the received signals are of adequate strength and coherence, and a memory mode when these conditions do not exist.

The frequency of operation is between 8·7 and 8·9 GHz and pulse repetition frequency is 50 kHz, with a pulse width having a mean value of 0·9 μsec. The high value of the prf enables unambiguous determination of Doppler shift with aircraft speeds up to 700 knots (approximately 1300 km/hr). The peak power of the transmitter is 1100 W and the average power (nominal) is 50 W. The equipment can operate up to an altitude of 20,000 m.

7.8 Accuracy of Doppler Navigation Systems

The overall Doppler navigation system accuracy depends upon the accuracy of the measurement of ground speed and the heading accuracy. Computational error may be a factor of importance if analog computers are used, but the present tendency is to use digital computation, in which the computational errors can be reduced to negligible proportions. The earlier systems had an overall accuracy of position better than 1% of the distance travelled over fairly long distances. It is expected that with improved heading references and negligible computational error, this may be reduced to 0·25% of the distance travelled.

8

Inertial Navigation

INERTIAL navigation is a system of dead-reckoning navigation in which the instruments in the craft determine its acceleration and by successive integration, obtain its velocity and displacement. The system is entirely self-contained and can be used both on earth, under the sea and in space. Its earliest use appears to have been in nuclear-powered submarines. The earlier equipment was bulky and heavy but subsequent developments have reduced the size and weight to such an extent that it is now being used in some aircraft. The principal advantages of the inertial system are its self-contained nature, immunity from jamming, absence of any radiation and the fact that it is useable at all latitudes. It has a high degree of accuracy, though, like all dead reckoning systems, its accuracy decreases with time.

8.1 Principles of Operation

The essential elements of the inertial navigator are *accelerometers* which determine the acceleration of the craft and a set of *gyroscopes* which maintain the directions of these accelerations along the desired coordinates. In addition, a computer is required to integrate the acceleration with respect to time, to obtain the velocity of the craft and the distance it has travelled along the chosen coordinates.

For simplicity, let us consider first navigation in space free from gravitational field. Let x_1, x_2 and x_3 represent the positions of the vehicle in a set of orthogonal cartesian coordinates fixed with reference to the 'fixed stars'. Such a set of coordinates is called an inertial frame of reference. The three components of acceleration are then $\ddot{x}_1$, $\ddot{x}_2$ and $\ddot{x}_3$ (where each dot represents a differentiation with respect to time). If these accelerations are determined, the position of the vehicle at any time t can be determined thus:

$$\text{velocity} = \dot{x}_1(t) = \int_0^t \ddot{x}(t)\ dt + \dot{x}_1(0)$$

$$\text{displacement} = x_1(t) = \int_0^t \dot{x}_1(t)dt + x(0)$$

$$= \int_0^t [\int_0^t \ddot{x}_1(t)dt]\ dt + \dot{x}_1(0)t + x_1(0)$$

$$8.1$$

where $(\dot{x}_1)(0)$ and $x_1(0)$ are respectively the initial velocity and position along the x_1 axis. In a similar manner, $x_3(t)$ and $x_3(t)$ can be determined. Note that the above expressions imply that the initial velocity and position are known.

The presence of a gravitational field changes the situation. The vehicle then accelerates under the influence of both the gravitational force and its own thrust. Accelerometers (Sec. 8.3.1) do not respond to gravitational forces as there act both on the case of the accelerometers and on the 'proof mass' inside them. The thrust of the vehicle acts on the case of the accelerometer, which is attached to the body of the vehicle, but not on the proof mass and consequently the accelerometers respond to the thrust acceleration. However, if gravitational acceleration is known, it may be taken into account and the true acceleration of the vehicle in the inertial frame of reference may be determined. Eqs. 8.1 then become applicable. In general, it can be assumed that the gravitational acceleration can be computed if the position of the vehicle in the inertial frame of reference is known. The block diagram in Fig. 8.1 illustrates the inertial navigation system in its most general form.

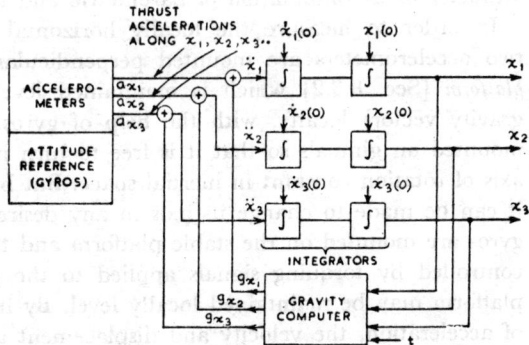

Fig. 8.1 Block diagram of the general inertial naviga-tion system

The input to the integrators in this case is the sum of the thrust acceleration a_x and the gravitational acceleration g_x along the particular axis. The compo-nents of gravitational acceleration are, in turn, computed from the position of the vehicle and time. This last factor is to take account of the fact that the gravitational field at any point changes with time. The 'attitude reference' consists of a set of gyros which maintain the orientation of the accelerometers along the required axes. This general block diagram may be modified to take into account the requirements of particular situations.

8.2 Navigation Over the Earth

We are interested here principally in navigation of a craft over earth either on the surface of the earth as in the case of sea-going vessels or close to the earth as in the case of aircraft. Navigation over the earth presents the following features:

(1) The system of coordinates should be fixed with reference to earth. As earth is rotating, the system of axes fixed with respect to earth is a non-inertial system. (The orbital motion of the earth does not make it a non-inertial system, as the orbital motion is one of 'free fall' under the influence of gravitational forces. A system of axes centred at the earth and fixed with reference to the fixed stars, is an inertial system of axes.)

(2) The coordinate system most convenient for use is latitude and longitude, which constitute a set of curvilinear coordinates on a spheroidal surface.

(3) A very large gravitational field is present at the surface of the earth.

For navigation over the earth, the inertial system is made to compute two components of acceleration which are locally horizontal. The vertical component is not generally used, as instrumentation for vertical motion by inertial means leads to exponentially increasing errors. Alternative methods of computing the vertical motion have to be employed, such as the barometric altimeter or a combination of barometric and inertial systems.[20]

In order to measure the locally horizontal components of acceleration, two accelerometers are mounted perpendicular to each other on a *stable platform* [Sec. 8.3.2] which is maintained level (i.e. perpendicular to the gravity vector) locally, with the help of gyros. Normally, a gyro which is mounted on gimbals so that it is free to turn in any direction maintains its axis of rotation constant in inertial space. But by applying a suitable torque, it can be made to change its axis in any desired manner. [Sec. 8.3.2]. The gyros are mounted on the stable platform and the orientation of the latter is controlled by torquing signals applied to the gyros. In this manner, the platform may be maintained locally level. By integration of the components of acceleration, the velocity and displacement along the desired coordinates are obtained. Before going into the details of the method, the components making up the system will be described.

8.3 Components of an Inertial Navigation System

8.3.1 Accelerometers

These instruments measure the thrust acceleration of the vehicle. Various types of accelerometers have been developed for inertial navigation. To illustrate the principle of operation of accelerometers in general, the simple arrangement shown in Fig. 8.2 will be considered. The accelerometer consists essentially of the body B, attached to the vehicle, and mass M called the

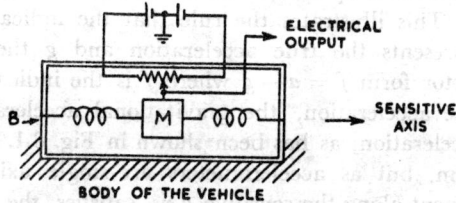

Fig. 8.2 A simple accelerometer

'proof mass' which is not rigidly fixed but is capable of frictionless movement along one axis of the body. This axis is called the 'sensitive axis'. The movement of the mass along this axis is constrained by springs which have one of their ends fixed to the body and the other to the mass. The forces acting on the vehicle due to the thrust act on the body but cannot act on the mass M, as it is a free mass and, therefore, it tends to remain in a state of rest or of uniform motion in a straight line. However, as it is constrained by the springs, it is forced to accelerate with the vehicle. In a state of equilibrium, the force exerted on the mass by the springs is proportional to the acceleration of the mass according to the relation

$$F = ma \qquad 8.2$$

where m is the mass of M and a its acceleration, which in the state of equilibrium is the acceleration of B or of the vehicle. The displacement of the mass from its equilibrium position is a measure of F. Knowing F and m, the acceleration can be determined. Fig. 8.2 shows an arrangement for obtaining an electrical output proportional to the displacement. Note that an acceleration to the right results in a displacement of the mass to the left within the body B and *vice versa*. Ideally, accelerometers should be insensitive to accelerations orthogonal to the sensitive axis.

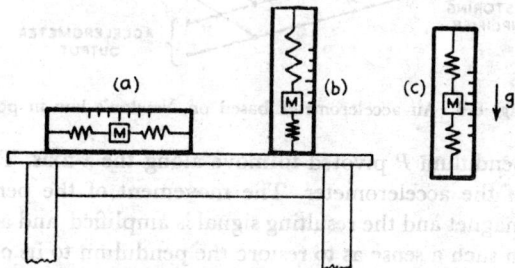

Fig. 8.3 Effect of gravity on the accelerometer output [(a) resting on table horizontal, (b)vertical, and (c) free fall]

Consider such an accelerometer in a state of rest on a table. If the sensitive axis is horizontal, no acceleration is indicated (Fig. 8.3). The component of g along the sensitive axis is then zero. If allowed to stand vertically, the mass moves down under the action of gravity and an upward acceleration $(-g)$ is indicated. If allowed to fall freely, the indicated acceleration is zero, while if accelerated upwards with an acceleration of magnitude $2g$, the indication is $3g$. This illustrates the rule that the indicated acceleration is $a-g$ where **a** represents the true acceleration and g the gravitational acceleration. In vector form $f = a - g$ where f is the indicated acceleration. To obtain the true acceleration, the gravitational acceleration is added to the indicated acceleration, as has been shown in Fig. 8.1. The above equation is in vector form, but as accelerometers are single axis devices, the appropriate component along the sensitive axis satisfies the above equation.

The accelerometer discussed above is not a practical one and is given for purposes of illustration. But many accelerometers in use make use of Newton's law $F = ma$ in some form. A common variant is Newton's law in its polar form

$$T = I\ddot{\theta} \qquad 8.3$$

where T is the torque, I the moment of inertia and $\ddot{\theta}$ the angular acceleration of the body. In addition, in practice, the moving body is not allowed to move but is restored to its normal position by a feed-back system which causes a force (or a torque) to be exerted on the mass electromagnetically. The magnitude of this restoring force is then a measure of the acceleration. One such system[20] is illustrated in Fig. 8.4. Here, the proof mass is provided by the

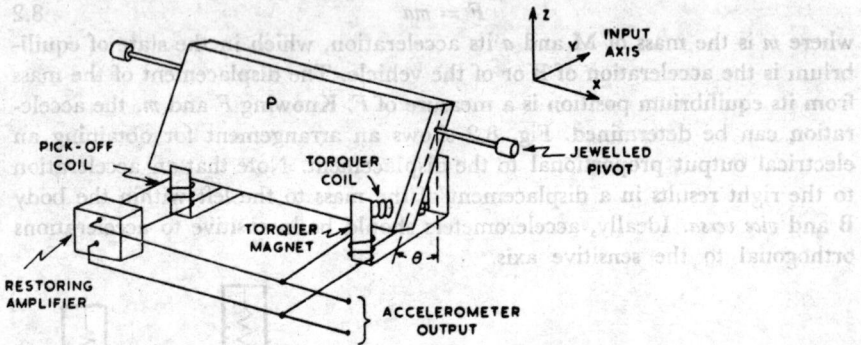

Fig. 8.4 An accelerometer based on Newton's law in polar form

pendulum P pivoted to move along the x-axis. The Y-axis is the sensitive axis of the accelerometer. The movement of the pendulum is sensed by pick-off magnet and the resulting signal is amplified and applied to the torquer magnet in such a sense as to restore the pendulum to its original position. In the steady state, the pendulum attains a position which is slightly displaced from its equilibrium position in the absence of acceleration and the restoring force which is proportional to the displacement, is such as to exactly balance the force due to acceleration. This relation may be put in the form

$$k\theta = mbf_y \qquad 8.4$$

where

mb = pendulosity of the moving part (g-cm)

f_y = the component of the acceleration along the y-axis (or sensitive axis)

θ = the small displacement of the pendulum and

k = a constant which takes into account the servo-amplifier gain and any spring stiffness that may be present.

The restoring amplifier output gives $k\theta$ and f_y may, therefore, be obtained. The above equation ignores all complicating factors such as the residual torque due to connecting wires, the effect of cross-axis acceleration, etc.

Another type of accelerometer employs two vibrating strings with a proof mass at the centre. In the absence of acceleration, the tensions of the two strings are equal and their frequencies of oscillation are the same (Fig. 8.5).

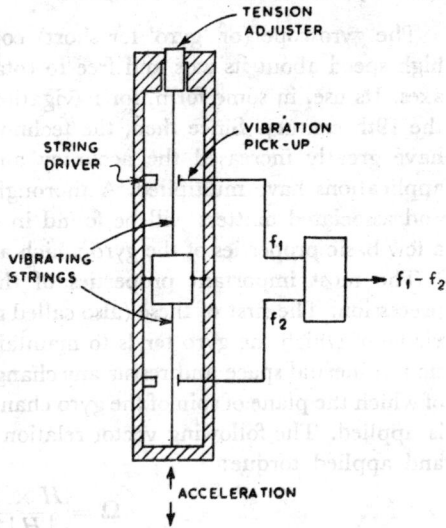

Fig. 8.5 Vibrating string accelerometer

The frequency of oscillation of each string is proportional to the square root of the tension of the spring. In the presence of an acceleration along the sensitive axis (which is coincident with the string) the tension on one is reduced and on the other is increased by the same amount. If the initial tension is T_0, the two frequencies in the presence of an acceleration a are:

frequency of the 1st string $= f_1 = k_1 \sqrt{T_0 + \Delta T}$

frequency of the 2nd string $= f_2 = k_1 \sqrt{T_0 - \Delta T}$

and $f_1 - f_2 = k_1 \sqrt{T_0}\left[\frac{\Delta T}{T_0} + \frac{1}{8}\left(\frac{\Delta T}{T_0}\right)^3 + \ldots \right]$ 8.5

where $\Delta T \propto ma$ = proof mass × axial acceleration.

If T_0 is large compared with the changes in tension ΔT brought about by the acceleration, the difference frequency is proportional to the acceleration. If a higher accuracy is required, the other terms in the bracket can be used as correction terms in the computation of velocity and displacement. The design of these accelerometers must ensure that the support of the proof mass is such that only its acceleration along the sensitive axis affects the tension of the strings. Vibrating string accelerometers tend to exhibit sensitivity to cross-axis acceleration and to vibration. The main advantage of these devices is that the integration of acceleration is easily implemented by a counter which counts the number of cycles of the difference frequency in a given time.[26]

A third type of accelerometer employs a gyroscope with an unbalance. The precession of such a gyro is a measure of the acceleration. The actual rotation is a measure of the integral of acceleration, i.e. the velocity. This type of gyro is called the unbalanced integrating gyro. For details of this type of accelerometer Ref. 25 may be seen.

8.3.2   Gyros and Stabilized Platforms

The gyroscope (or 'gyro' for short) consists of a heavy rotor spinning at a high speed about its axis and free to rotate about one or more perpendicular axes. Its use, in some form, for navigational purposes appears to date back to the 19th century. Since then, the technology of gyro design and construction have greatly increased the accuracy and reliability of the device and its applications have multiplied. A thorough treatment of gyrosopic phenomena and associated matters will be found in Ref. 27, 28. We will deal here with a few basic properties of the gyro which are made use of in inertial navigation.

The most important properties of the gyro are gyroscopic inertia and precession. The first of these (also called gyroscopic rigidity) is the property by virtue of which the gyro tends to maintain its axis of rotation in a fixed direction in inertial space and resists any change. Precession is the property by virtue of which the plane of spin of the gyro changes at a constant rate when a torque is applied. The following vector relation holds between the rate of precession and applied torque:

$$\Omega = \frac{H \times T}{|H|^2} \tag{8.6}$$

where Ω is the angular velocity of precession, H, the angular momentum of the body, (= moment of inertia I × spin rate ω_s), and T, the applied torque. This relation is illustrated in Fig. 8.6 where the torque and spin are orthogonal. When the spin is along the Y-axis and a torque is along the X-axis, the gyro precesses about the Z-axis, as shown in 8.6(a). (The precession is in a direction which tends to make the spin axis coincide with the torque.) Conversely, when the gyro is made to precess in the Z-axis, this causes a torquing force to appear along the X-axis [Fig. 8.6(b)]. With a constant applied torque, the precession is constant or the axis of spin rotates at a constant rate. This is in contrast to what happens in the case of a non-spinning mass, where the application of a torque would make the body rotate at a linearly increasing rate.

The gyro is mounted on gimbals, as shown in Fig. 8.7 so that its spin axis may be rotated about one or two other axes. The figure shows a gyro which is capable of rotation about two axes. The mass spins about the Z-axis on

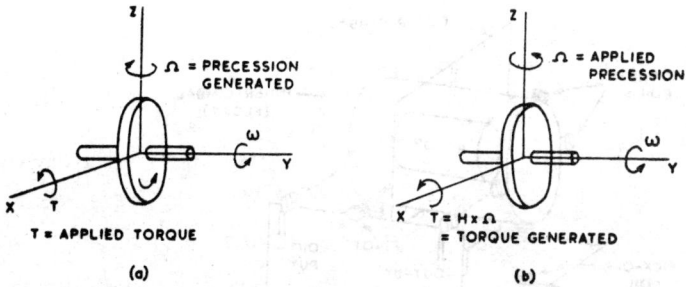

Fig. 8.6 Effects of torque and precession in a gyroscope

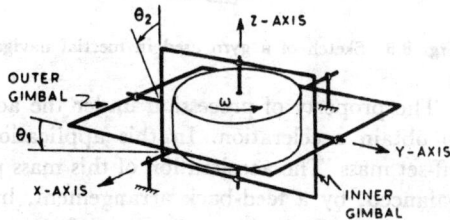

Fig. 8.7 Two-degree-of-freedom gyro

bearings fixed to the inner gimbal, the inner gimbal itself can rotate about the Y-axis on bearings fixed to the outer gimbal, which in turn can rotate about the X-axis on bearings fixed to the frame. Such a gyro is called a two-degree-of-freedom gyro. If the outer gimbal is fixed to the frame, only rotation about the Y-axis is possible and the gyro is called a single-degree-of-freedom gyro. This can sense the rotation of the frame along one axis. Three such gyros are required to sense the rotation along three axes. In navigational applications, the property of gyroscopic rigidity is not used directly, but small changes in the orientation of the gyro axis in relation to the gimbals is electrically sensed and a feed-back arrangement is used to precess the gyro in some desired manner. In this way, the gyro may be constrained to take up certain fixed orientation, say, in earth coordinates rather than in inertial coordinates.

The modern gyro used for navigational purposes is a device of very high precision. Its spinning mass is electrically driven and is the rotor of an electric motor. To obtain a high degree of gyroscopic rigidity, the moment of inertia and angular velocity have to be high. The rotor is designed to have most of the mass concentrated near the periphery and speeds of rotation may be as high as 30,000 rev/min. The older gyros operated with ball bearings but later ones have self-lubricated gas bearings.[20] The rotor and the stator are usually mounted within a float which serves as the inner gimbal (Fig. 8.8). The outer gimbal is filled with a fluid of such a specific gravity that the weight of the float is compensated. This reduces the load on gimbal bearings. Two sets of pick-off coils are provided for sensing any small rotation about the gimbal axis and two sets of coils are provided for applying the torque ('torquer coils') to bring about the desired precession.

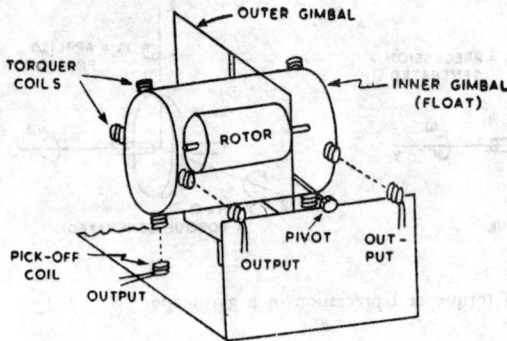

Fig. 8.8   Sketch of a gyro used in inertial navigation

The property of precession under the action of a torque may be employed to obtain acceleration. In this application, the gyro is unbalanced by an off-set mass. The acceleration of this mass produces a torque, which is counter balanced, by a feed-back arrangement, by precessing the gyro. The precessional rate (Ω) is then a measure of the acceleration ar. ' 'he angle precessed is proportional to the integral of acceleration, or velocity. Such gyros are called *integrating gyro accelerometers*. These are not generally used for navigation but find application in ballistic missiles.

Stable platforms serve the purpose of isolating the inertial sensing elements, such as the accelerometers, from vehicle motion. The stabilized platform is mounted on gimbals to permit rotation of the vehicle with respect to the platform along the three axes. The platform is maintained at the desired orientation by gimbal servos which are actuated by error signals produced by gyros whenever there is a deviation of the orientation from the desired one. The three possible angular errors may be sensed either by two two-degree-of-freedom gyros or three single-degree-of-freedom gyros.

The gimbal system may be external or internal to the stable mount (or stable element). In the former, the stable element is surrounded by an inner gimbal to which the stable element is pivoted along one axis, the inner gimbal is pivoted to the second one along an axis at right angles to the first axis, and the second gimbal is pivoted to the third one along an axis perpendicular to the two former ones. In aircraft installations, where the vehicle may pitch or roll by large angles, a fourth or redundant gimbal may be used. This is to eliminate the possibility of 'gimbal lock' which occurs when the vehicle pitches by large angles. Under conditions of gimbal lock, one degree of freedom is lost. This is illustrated in Fig. 8.9(a) which shows a three gimbal system in an aircraft in level flight (i) and when the aircraft has turned by 90° about the roll axis (ii). Two axes coincide in the latter case and the gimbal system is unable to cope with movement about the pitch axis. With four gimbals, as shown in 8.9(b), movement about the three axes is always possible by suitable use of the redundant gimbal. In Fig. 8.9(b), the vehicle is shown

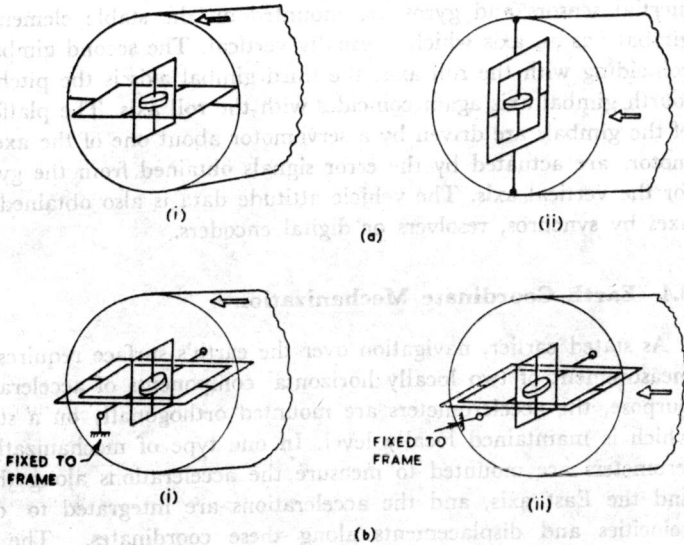

(i)
(a)
(ii)

(i)
FIXED TO FRAME
(ii)
FIXED TO FRAME
(b)

Fig. 8.9 Gimbal lock [(a) three-gimbal mount, (b) four-gimbal mount]

both in the normal position (i) and with near 90° roll angle (ii). When the roll exceeds a certain amount, the fourth gimbal motor takes over and turns the second gimbal to a level position. Thus, the first two gimbals are maintained orthogonal. For further details of the fourth gimbal operation, see Ref. 20, 29. The four gimbal system is invariably used in aircraft when pitch and roll angles approaching 90° are likely during maneuvers. In ships and passenger aircraft, where this possibility does not exist, a three-gimbal system may be used. The third gimbal in the latter is replaced by the mounting structure for the platform in the carrying vehicle.

A four-axis stable platform is shown diagramatically in Fig. 8.10. The

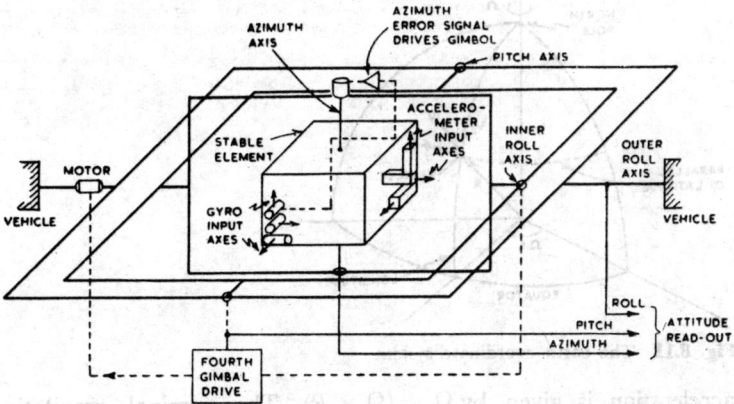

Fig. 8.10 A four-axis stable platform

inertial sensors and gyros are mounted on the stable element. The inner gimbal has an axis which is usually vertical. The second gimbal has an axis coinciding with the roll axis, the third gimbal axis is the pitch axis and the fourth gimbal axis again coincides with the roll axis. The platform and each of the gimbals are driven by a servomotor about one of the axes. The servo-motors are actuated by the error signals obtained from the gyros, as shown for the vertical axis. The vehicle attitude data is also obtained for the three axes by synchros, resolvers or digital encoders.

8.4   Earth Coordinate Mechanization

As stated earlier, navigation over the earth's surface requires basically the measurement of two locally horizontal components of acceleration. For this purpose, the accelerometers are mounted orthogonally on a stable platform which is maintained locally level. In one type of mechanization, the acce-lerometers are mounted to measure the accelerations along the North axis and the East axis, and the accelerations are integrated to determine the velocities and displacements along these coordinates. The latitude and longitude are then obtained directly. The gyros are precessed continuously to maintain the platform level and to keep the accelerometers pointing North and East. The signals necessary for precessing the gyros are computed, in turn, from position and velocity information.

The movement of a vehicle on a rotating earth gives rise to some fictitious (or apparent) accelerations called Coriolis accelerations which have to be allowed for to obtain the true acceleration of the vehicle in earth coordinates. In addition to this, centripetal acceleration is also present. If R is the vector representing the position of the object with respect to the centre of the earth (Fig. 8.11) as origin, and Ω the angular velocity of the earth, the centripetal

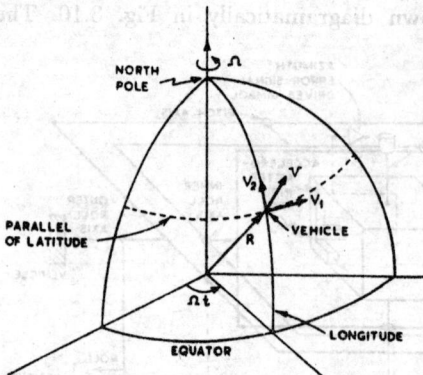

Fig. 8.11 The earth coordinate system

acceleration is given by $\Omega \times (\Omega \times R)$. The nominal gravitational acce-leration at the surface of the earth which we have previously considered is the true (Newtonian) gravitational acceleration minus the centripetal acceleration and is the usual definition of gravitational acceleration. Taking these factors into consideration, the acceleration of the vehicles is given in vector form by[20,25]

$$\frac{dV}{dt}\bigg|_p = U - (\omega + \Omega) \times V + g \qquad\qquad 8.7$$

$$g = G - \Omega \times (\Omega \times R)$$

where V = ground velocity of the vehicle,

$\dfrac{dV}{dt}\bigg|_p$ = vector derivative of V in platform coordinates (Northward,

         Eastward and upwards in the case considered above),

    G = Newtonian gravitational acceleration,

    U = Acceleration vector measured by the accelerometers,

    ω = inertial angular velocity of the platform,

    Ω = inertial angular velocity of the earth, and

    g = gravitational acceleration (with a locally horizontal platform, this is normal to the platform and has no components along the latitude and longitude).

The vector equation may be reduced to three scalar equations, of which the two relating to the motion of vehicle in the horizontal plane are usually solved for navigational purposes. Indicating by subscripts 1, 2, and 3, the components along the East, North and upward axes, these two relevant equations take the following form:

$$\left.\begin{aligned}
\frac{dV_1}{dt} &= u_1 - \{(w_2 + \Omega_2) V_3 - (w_3 + \Omega_3) V_1\} \\
\frac{dV_2}{dt} &= u_2 - \{(w_3 + \Omega_3) V_1 - (w_1 + \Omega_1) V_3\}
\end{aligned}\right\} \qquad 8.8$$

Here, u_1 and u_2 are the accelerations measured by the accelerometers and the term within the brackets represents the Coriolis corrections. The accelerations given by the left hand side of the equations are integrated to obtain velocity and displacement along the latitude and longitude. The mechanization of these equations is illustrated in Fig. 8.12. The various computations indicated may be performed by a single computer in practice. Note that the position and velocity are used to compute the gyro precession commands.

The various quantities involved in the computations are as follows.

$$\left.\begin{aligned}
\Omega_1 &= 0 & \omega_1 &= \Omega_1 - \frac{V_2}{R_M + h} \\
\Omega_2 &= \Omega \cos\phi & \omega_2 &= \Omega_2 + \frac{V_1}{(R_P + h)\cos\phi} \\
\Omega_3 &= \Omega \sin\phi & \omega_3 &= \omega_2 \sin\phi
\end{aligned}\right\} \qquad 8.9$$

where

    ϕ = latitude of the vehicle,

    R_M = radius of curvature of the earth in the meridian plane,

    R_p = radius of curvature of the earth in the East-West vertical plane, and

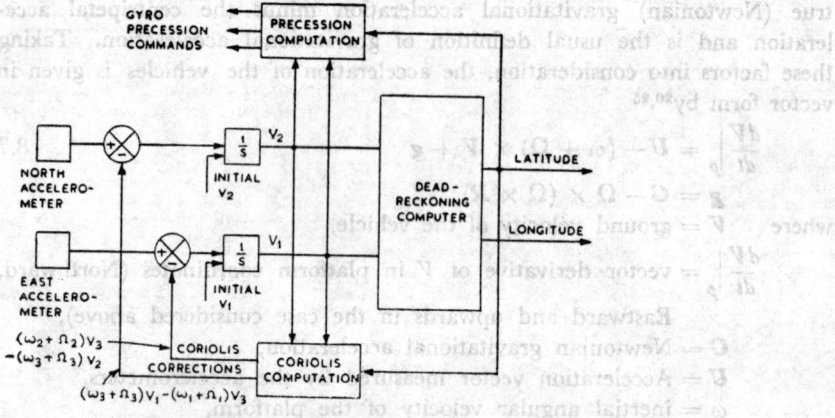

Fig. 8.12 Mechanization for navigation in the latitude longitude system of coordinates

$$h = \text{altitude of the vehicle.}$$

The mechanization described above is the simplest conceptually and is suitable for use up to moderate latitudes. It is unsatisfactory at high latitudes, as the computation of longitude (or V_1) becomes inaccurate as ϕ approaches 90°. This is seen from Eq. 8.9, in which ω_2 has a term involving the reciprocal of cos ϕ. Further, the gyro torquing rates become excessive at high latitudes. Other types of mechanization are possible, one of which is the 'free-azimuth' or the "wander azimuth" system where the platform is not precessed for azimuth but account is taken of wander angle in the computation. This system has some advantages over the system with a North-pointing platform and can be operated at all latitudes.[20]

8.5   Strapped-Down Systems

A system of mechanization of inertial navigation which does not use the stable platform is possible. In this system the accelerometers are mounted on the vehicle and are, therefore, fixed to the vehicle coordinate system. The accelerations measured are then in vehicle coordinates. These are then processed in a computer along with the vehicle attitude data derived from a system of gyros to obtain the velocity and displacement in any desired coordinate system. At the present stage of development, strapped-down systems are not accurate enough for navigation over appreciable periods of time and are used mainly in missiles.

8.6   Accuracy of Inertial Navigation Systems

Total system accuracy of inertial navigators is high and is likely to increase with advances in technology. The errors, as in other dead-reckoning systems, increase with time. They arise from various causes such as gyro-drift, accelerometer errors, linearity and scale factor errors of the gyro-torquer, computer errors and initial condition errors. Some errors are oscillatory and have periods of the earth rate Ω, the Schüler frequency $\omega_s = \sqrt{g/R}$ (84·4 minute period) and a frequency $2 \Omega \sin \phi$. These frequencies arise out of the nature of the system mechanization.

Some reported values of error are in the range of 1 to 1·5 km for a flight period of 4 to 6 hr. Greater accuracies may still be expected, but there are some fundamental limits to the accuracy of an inertial navigation system. These arise mainly from the uncertainty of the gravitational field in the region of operation and angular errors arising from the precession of equinoxes and the migration of earth's poles.

9

Recent Developments & Trends

In the previous chapters, many of the navigational aids which are in use at present have been described. A number of other aids which are either in use or in development at present are given in Appendix IV. In this chapter, we consider some navigational aids that are emerging and discuss the trends in the future requirements of navigation.

The needs of navigation, particularly of air navigation, have changed considerably over the last two decades and some of the factors which are responsible for this are as follows:

(1) Increase in air-traffic densities and the requirement for more precise position fixing to avoid risk of collision.

(2) The increasing use of long routes over the sea as in North Atlantic.

(3) The increasing speed of aircraft, necessitating continuous position information rather than intermittent fixes.

In the past, navigation has almost always involved a human operator or observer who takes intermittent fixes. The present trend in advanced aircraft is to employ a computer, to obtain continuous position information as the delays inevitable with a human operator may not be tolerable. A computer is invariably involved in Doppler and inertial navigation as we have seen. This may be a special purpose computer for the particular navigational aid. Alternatively, a computer which performs a multiplicity of tasks, such as monitoring the state of aircraft dynamics in addition to performing navigational computations may be employed.

When a computer with sufficient capacity is available, it may be employed for optimum utilization of navigational data. The use of more than one navigational facility has of course been common practice, particularly the combination of dead-reckoning with intermittent fixes obtained by other means like the celestial fix. In such cases, the position is updated by that facility which is considered to be more accurate. This means, in effect, that 100% weightage is given to the intermittent fix and no weightage to the dead-reckoning fix. But when two facilities are of comparable accuracy, weightage has to be given in an optimal manner, i.e. in a way which minimizes the probable error. For this purpose, new techniques involving Kalman filtering[30] have been used, for the implementation of which a digital computer is necessary.

Another aspect of navigation is the coverage provided by navigational aids over long routes, particularly intercontinental routes over the sea. Most of the radio facilities considered in earlier chapters have a limited range. Those available all over the world are celestial navigation and self-contained systems such as Doppler and inertial navigation. The latter two being dead-reckoning systems, their accuracy degrades with time and periodic checks are necessary. Lately, celestial navigation has been made more accurate and automatic by the development of star-trackers[20]. Two new radio aids have come into existence, which promise to provide worldwide coverage. These are the *Omega*, a very low frequency hyperbolic system, and *satellite navigation system*. A brief account of these are given in the next two sections.

9.1 The Omega System

This is a hyperbolic system which works in the very low frequency region (around 10 kHz) and has a very long base line of the order of 7000 km. The principle underlying the system is the same as in other hyperbolic systems, namely the measurement of the difference in path length to two or more fixed stations, which defines a locus. As in Decca, the difference in the phases of the signal from two stations gives the position lines. In addition, the phases of the transmission are controlled very precisely in standard time and, therefore, the comparison of the phase of the signal with a precision phase source in the receiver can give the radial distance from a station.

Each station transmits a signal precisely controlled in time and frequency according to the order shown in Fig. 9.1. Each transmission of 11·33, 13·6 and 10·2 kHz is approximately of one sec. duration and between transmissions there is a gap of about 0·2 sec. The cycle repeats with a period of 10 sec and in the period not covered by the above frequencies, a characteristic carrier is transmitted by each station. The three one-second transmissions are phase modulated by a low frequency for lane identification and transmission of standard time. At each half min. of standard time, all carrier and modulation frequency currents pass through zero with a positive slope. As the transmissions have this relation to standard time, no master or slave relationship is necessary. At the receiver, the phase of the signal is 'remembered' by circuits to compare the phase difference between the transmission of two stations at each frequency at different times. The phase difference gives the position within a lane. Lane identification is accomplished by phase comparison at the difference frequencies of 3·4 kHz, and 1·13 kHz, i.e. (13·6-10·2) and

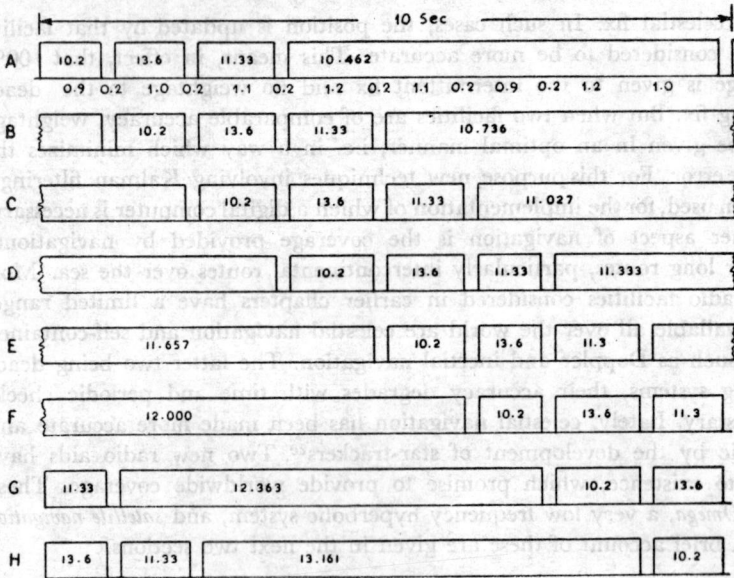

Fig. 9.1   Transmissions of the stations of Omega system

(11·33-10·2) kHz respectively. Navigation with one receiver for 10·2 kHz is also possible if other facilities can be utilized.

The omega system is subject to errors, some of which are predictable and some are random. Allowing for predictable errors, positional accuracies of 2 km are possible.

9.2   Satellite Navigation Systems

This may be regarded as an extension of celestial navigation, as satellites have predictable orbits. They have an advantage over the celestial body in that the satellite can radiate an rf transmission and may also carry a transponder beacon and can provide all-weather service.

Satellites for navigation can be of two types, low altitude ones with orbital periods of the order of 100 min. and 'synchronous' satellites with a period of one sidereal day, in a geo-stationary orbit. The latter type appear to be stationary over some point on the equator. One of the earliest satellites for navigation was a non-synchronous satellite (called 'Transit') with polar orbit employed by the U.S Navy for accurate position fixing of Polaris missile-carrying submarines. Many later proposals and designs envisage systems of synchronous satellites.

The use of the satellite for navigation may be based on several different techniques. The first, which may be called the *angle-only* system, envisages the determination of the elevation angle of the satellite, and is an obvious extension of celestial navigation. However, determination of the angle of arrival of the radiation emitted by the satellite cannot be very accurate unless impractically large antennas are used. An alternative to this is the measurement of the angle of arrival of the emission from the ground by employing interferometric techniques in the satellite. A pair of such antennas on the satellite may be able to provide adequately accurate angle measurements. Measurement of two angles in planes perpendicular to each other would be sufficient to give a fix to the craft. This system would require communication between the satellite and aircraft.

The first satellite to be used for navigation employed a different principle, that of determining the 'Doppler profile'. This method is also called the 'range rate system'. Basically, the system consists of one or more satellites whose orbital position is precisely known, giving a continuous emission at a known frequency. The receiver in the craft records the frequency history of the received signal. As the distance from the satellite to the craft decreases, there is a positive Doppler shift, which reduces to zero at the minimum distance and becomes negative as the satellite recedes. A plot of the Doppler shift against time is called the Doppler profile. A single such profile is capable of giving the position information. The time at which the Doppler shift is zero and the slope of the profile at that point uniquely determine the position of the aircraft. Fig. 9.2 indicates how the Doppler profile changes with the position of the aircraft.

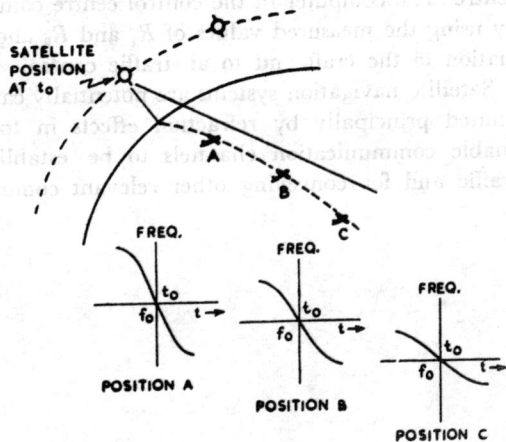

Fig. 9.2 Velocity profiles obtained with the range-rate system

The systems at present under development envisage synchronous satellites in equatorial orbit. The measurement of distance from the satellites and in some cases, the angle of the satellite could be made. Secondary radar may be used for the former. In one proposed system (Fig. 9.3), a ground control centre sends coded signals to the craft via two or more satellites and a

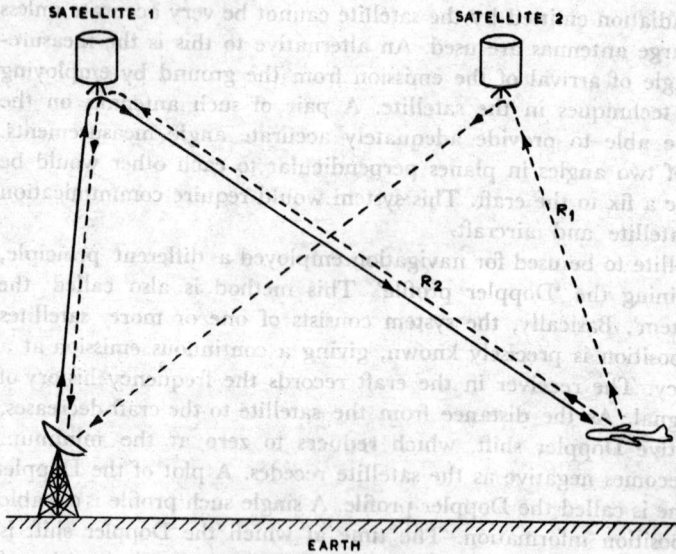

Fig. 9.3 A scheme for navigation using synchronous satellites

transponder in the craft returns these signals via the satellite to the control centre. The computer in the control centre computes the position of the craft by using the measured values of R_1 and R_2 and transmits the position information to the craft and to air-traffic control.

Satellite navigation systems are potentially capable of high accuracy, being limited principally by refraction effects in the atmosphere. Satellites also enable communication channels to be established to help control of air traffic and for conveying other relevant commercial data.

APPENDIX I

Maps & Charts

THE FIRST need of a navigator is a map of the region he is going to traverse, wherefrom he can get a knowledge of the position of departure and destination as well as of the intervening terrain. The maps used for navigation are generally called 'charts' and are printed to various scales to suit a variety of navigational requirements.

The production of a map or a chart presents the problem of representing the spherical (or near-spherical) surface of the earth on a plane. A spherical surface is 'non-developable'. i.e. it cannot be spread out on a plane surface without distortion. Any method of representation of the spherical surface on a plane may be reduced to that of representing the parallels of latitude and the meridians of longitude by lines or curves, having a one-to-one correspondence with them, on a plane. These methods (there are many such methods) are called 'projections'. A projection can be 'perspective' or 'non-perspective'. The former is one in which the points on the globe are projected on to the desired surface by joining them to a point (called the origin) and projecting the line until it intersects the desired surface. This is also the sense in which the word perspective is commonly understood. The point of origin may be anywhere, even at infinity, but in the more common projections is at the centre of the globe. Non-perspective projections are modifications of perspective projections designed to represent some particular aspects of the region being projected, such as area, shape, etc.

All projections are compromises, as they cannot represent the spherical surface accurately in all respects. Some of the important factors to be considered in choosing a projection are: (a) the position of the region in relation to the earth's surface, (b) the direction which any point bears in relation to another, (c) the distance between any two given points in the region, (d) the shape of the region and (e) the accuracy with which the area is represented. All the above requirements are not satisfied by any projection and a choice has therefore, to be made keeping in mind the special requirements of any particular application. For navigation, factors (b) and (c) are important. The commonly used projections employed for navigational charts are the Mercator's, Lambert's and Gnomonic projections. Before proceeding to a description of these, it is to be noted that there are two types of routes which can be taken by a craft in going from one point to another on the globe. One is the great circle path, which is the shortest distance between the two points and the other is the rhumb line, which is the line which cuts the meridians at a constant angle. Over short distances (up to 300 or 500 km), there is little difference between the two paths. A rhumb line would be followed if a vehicle navigates by the compass and keeps the compass reading constant.

Mercator's Projections

This projection, which is the most widely used one in marine navigation, is obtained by projecting the points on the globe on to the surface of a cylinder having its axis coincident with axis of the globe. When the surface of the cylinder is 'developed', the parallels of latitude and the meridians appear as sets of parallel lines orthogonal to each other (Fig. I.1). In this projection, the

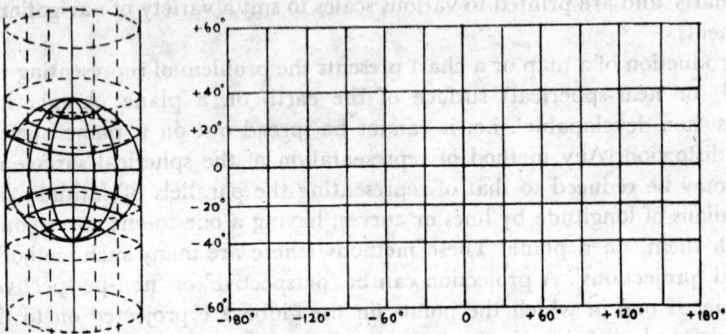

Fig. I.1 Mercator's projection

distance between the parallels of latitude increases rapidly as one moves towards the poles, and the linear distance from the equator to a parallel is made to increase at such a rate that the scale along a meridian is the same as the scale along the parallel *at that point*. The poles can never appear on this projection. The advantage of Mercator's projection is that a straight line connecting any two points is a rhumb line. The shapes of small areas are well preserved at all latitudes but the scale increases with latitude and, therefore, large areas particularly at the higher latitudes, appear distorted.

Mercator's projection is useful when navigation along a rhumb line is adequate, which is generally true for short distances. For navigation over long distances when the great circle path is to be followed, the desired route (which need not be straight on Mercator's projection) is determined by other means and is broken up into a number of segments and rhumb lines are substituted for these. Navigation can then be done by maintaining the required constant bearings over the segments.

Lambert's Conformal Conic or Lambert Projection

In this projection, a cone coaxial with the earth's axis is made to intersect the globe at two parallels of latitude, which are referred to as 'standard parallels'. The simple perspective conic projection is a special case of this, when the two standard parallels coincide. When developed, the Lambert projection yields a map in which the meridians are convergent lines (usually converging well outside the map) and the parallels of latitude appear as arcs of concentric circles. (Fig. I.2). The advantages of the Lambert projection are that even

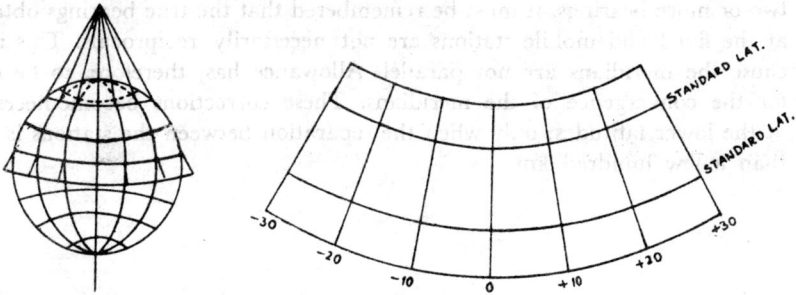

Fig. I.2 Lambert's projection

over a fairly large area (as for example the U.S.A.), a line joining two points is very close to the great circle and the angular representation is preserved. The bearing of one station from another can, therefore, be read off with a protractor. Lambert projection is widely used in charts for aeronautical navigation.

Gnomonic Projection

This is a perspective projection obtained by taking the centre of the globe as origin and projecting the points on it on to a plane tangential to the globe. All great circles will appear as straight lines and in particular, those passing through the point of contact form a set of radial lines (Fig. I.3). A common form of the gnomonic projection has the point of contact at the pole. The meridians, therefore, appear as radial lines and the parallels as concentric circles. A useful property of this gnomonic projection is that the bearing of all points from the point of contact are true. Though this projection is not used by itself for navigation, it is useful for determining the great circle route between any two points, which is simply the straight line joining the two points.

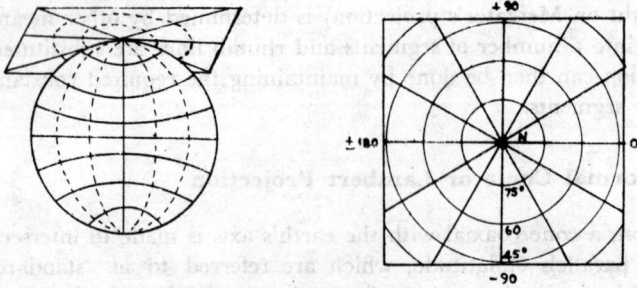

Fig. I.3 Gnomonic projection

The coordinates (latitudes and longitudes) of the points on this route can be found and transferred to any other desired projection.

When obtaining the bearing of a fixed station or when obtaining a fix from two or more bearings, it must be remembered that the true bearings obtained at the fixed and mobile stations are not necessarily reciprocals. This is because the meridians are not parallel. Allowance has, therefore, to be made for the convergence of the meridians. These corrections become necessary. at the lower latitudes, only when the separation between the stations is more than a few hundred km.

APPENDIX II

Multichannel Crystal Controlled Receivers

AIRCRAFT navigation and communication equipment, particularly the ones operating in the VHF band, are crystal-controlled. The allocated band is from about 108 to 136 MHz or more and the frequency separation of adjacent channels is 50 kHz. There are thus several hundred channels available within the band. It is advantageous to have fixed-tuned crystal-controlled receivers which can maintain stable tuning over long periods and eliminate the necessity for frequent adjustments. But if a single crystal is to be used for each channel, many hundreds of crystals are required for the whole band, which is a serious disadvantage from the point of view of the cost and the size of the equipment. On the other hand, the alternative of providing a limited number of channels which are most likely to be used, with provision for changing them, is also not desirable as it limits the usefulness of the equipment. Both these disadvantages are overcome in modern equipment by making provision for all the available channels with a limited number of crystals. This is achieved by the technique of multiple-heterodyning.

This technique, as applied to a receiver, consists in translating the VHF signal frequency to a low intermediate frequency (approximately 500 kHz) in successive steps, using crystal oscillators in each step. This is illustrated in Fig. II.1. The several oscillator frequency groups and the succeeding IF's must be so chosen as to ensure that there is no spurious response from frequencies within the band or outside it. It is clear from the figure that the final number (N) of channels obtainable is given by

$$N = n_1 \times n_2 \times n_3 \ldots \times n_r$$

where r is the number of steps of frequency translation. The number of crystals required (M, say) is

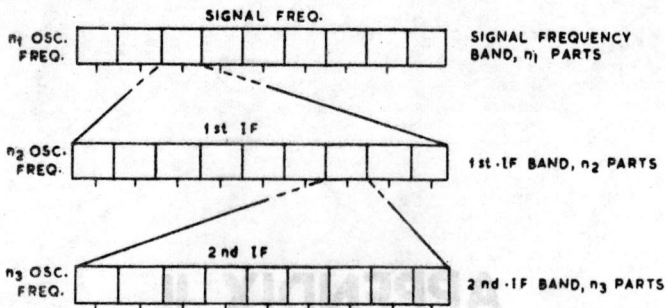

Fig. II.1 A scheme of multiple heterodyning

$$M = n_1 + n_2 + n_3 + \ldots + n_r$$

It can be shown that this is minimum, for a given N when

$$n_1 = n_2 = \ldots = n_r = n$$

which gives $\qquad N = n^r$ and $M = nr$.

For the minimum number of crystals, the value of n works out to be $\varepsilon\,(=$ $2 \cdot 7183\ldots)$, but even taking the nearest whole number of $n = 3$ often gives an impracticably large number of heterodyning steps. Taking, for example, $N = 2000$, if $n = 3$, then $r = 7(3^7 = 2187)$, i.e. seven heterodyning stages are required. The number of crystals required is 21. Whereas, if three steps of ten and one of two are used, the number of crystals required is 32, which is still not very large, but is certainly very small compared with 2000. In practice, therefore, the number of stages of heterodyning is made two or three and the number of frequencies in each step is made fairly large, generally 10 or 20.

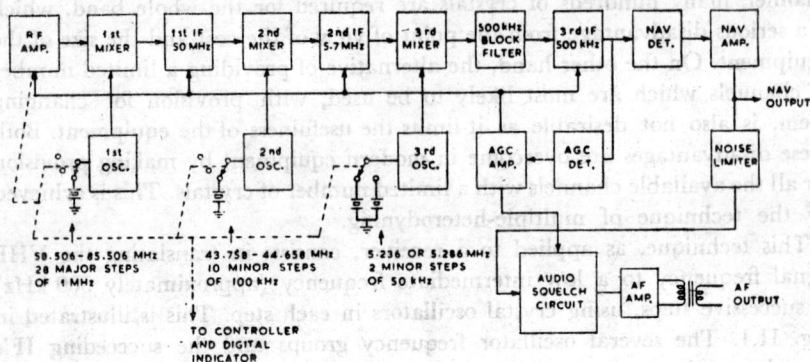

Fig. II.2 A 560-channel receiver (Marconi) using three stages of heterodyning

The block diagram of a receiver (Marconi AD 160) shown in Fig. II.2 employs such a scheme. The diagram is self-explanatory. Apart from the frequency selection scheme, note that there are two demodulated outputs, one for navigational purposes, and the other for audio. The former uses the full bandwidth while the latter has a filter (in the squelch circuit block) which limits the bandwidth to that required for radio telephony.

The principal disadvantage of the technique of multiple heterodyning is that it tends to increase the spurious frequency responses of the receiver. This has been sought to be overcome by an alternative scheme which employs a single stage of heterodyning followed (and proceeded) by highly selective filters.

APPENDIX III

Synchros & Resolvers

SYNCHROS and resolvers find application in many of the instrumentation
circuits of navigation equipment. A brief explanation of their principles is
given here. For more detailed information, see Ref. 31.

Synchros (also known by other trade names such as selsyns autosyns, etc.)
are devices which are used to convey angular position information from one
place to another by electrical means, thereby eliminating the need for any
mechanical linkage between the two points. The angular position of an 'input'
or 'control' shaft can be reproduced in an 'output' or 'load' shaft by the use
of synchros. If the load is very small, as is often the case with indicating
instruments, the synchro can directly operate the load shaft, but if considerable power is required, a feedback control system may be used in which the
synchro is employed to convey the output position data to the input point for
comparison and generation of error signals.

The synchro is a small ac machine which resembles a motor in construction.
It has a stator with three identical windings symmetrically positioned and a
rotor with a single winding. Several different types of synchros are used in
instrumentation, namely, synchro-generators, synchro-motors, and control-
transformers. Electrically, they are identical but there are some differences
in the construction of the motors and generators. Synchro differentials (both
generators and motors) are also used. These differ from the former electrically
in having three rotor windings, symmetrically positioned, instead of a single
one of the former.

The windings of a synchro generators are shown schematically in Fig. III.1.
An ac voltage E_R applied to the rotor winding R_1R_2 produces an alternating
magnetic field which induces voltages in the stator windings OS_1, OS_2 and
OS_3. By virtue of the construction of the synchro, each of these voltages will
be proportional to the cosine of the angle between the plane of the rotor and

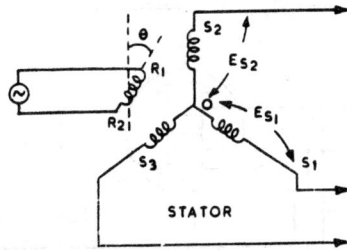

Fig. III.1
Schematic arrangement of a synchro

STATOR

of the corresponding stator. If θ is the angle between the plane of the rotor loop and that of OS_2 which we will take as reference, then the three voltages will be

$$E_{S_2} = KE_R \cos\theta.\cos\omega_s t$$
$$E_{S_1} = KE_R \cos(\theta - 120°).\cos\omega_s t$$
$$E_{S_3} = KE_R \cos(\theta - 240°).\cos\omega_s t$$

Where E_{S_1}, E_{S_2} and E_{S_3} are the voltages in the stators and K is a constant. Note that the three voltages are in phase but their peak amplitudes vary sinusoidally with the angle θ. The sum of the three voltages is easily shown to be zero. Also, if a symmetrical load is put on the stator, the rotor sees a constant load in all its positions.

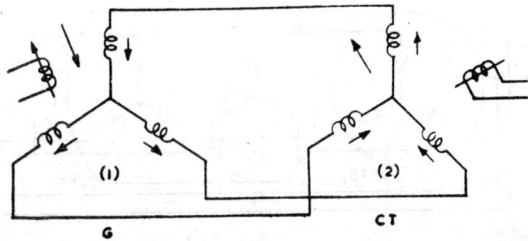

Fig. III.2 Sketch of a synchro-generator and control transformer

One form in which two synchros can be used is shown in Fig. III.2. Here, the stator of synchro 2 is the load for the stator of synchro 1. The ac voltage is applied to the rotor of No. 1, while the output is taken from the rotor of 2. In this configuration, the first one is called a synchro-generator and the second one a control-transformer. The currents in the stator coils of the control transformer are identical with the currents in those of the generator and, therefore, a field is produced in the control transformer which has the same orientation as the field in the transmitter, but is in the opposite direction. The voltage picked up by the rotor (open circuit) of the control transformer then varies sinusoidally with its orientation, being zero when its plane is parallel to the resultant magentic field. This property is made use of in servo systems by using the rotor output as the error signal.

Another common synchro configuration is shown in Fig. III.3. In this case, power is fed to the rotors of both the synchros. If the rotors are aligned and if

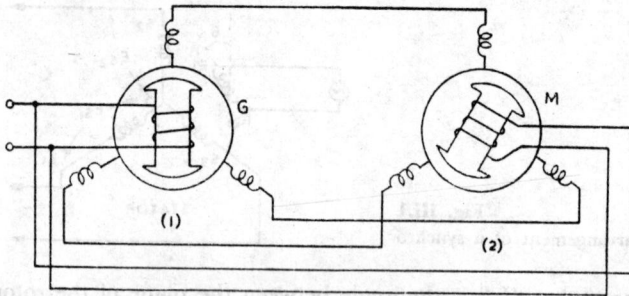

Fig. III.3 Sketch of torque-synchro

the voltages developed in the stators of the two synchros are equal, no current will flow and no torque will be developed. If they are not aligned, currents will flow and produce a torque in such a direction as to align the rotors. This type of arrangement is useful particularly when only a small torque is required, as in instrumentation. Synchros of this type are called torque-synchros. These devices provide a simple means of displaying the angular position of one rotor at a remote point, by installing a synchro-motor with an indicator needle.

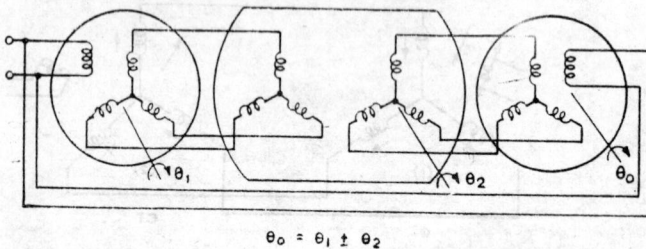

$$\theta_0 = \theta_1 \pm \theta_2$$

Fig. III.4 Sketch of a synchro-differential

The third configuration shown in Fig. III.4 employs a differential transmitter. As stated earlier, this has a rotor with three windings symmetrically disposed, which are Y-connected. It serves the purpose of a mechanical differential in giving the sum (or difference) of two angular inputs. A differential generator, for instance, has two inputs, an electrical one from a synchro corresponding to an angle θ_1 and a mechanical one in the form of its rotor position, say θ_2, and it gives an electrical output from its rotor corresponding to the angle $\theta_1 \pm \theta_2$. If this output is applied to the stator windings of a synchro to the rotor of which the ac supply is connected, then its rotor takes up a position corresponding to $\theta_0 = \theta_1 \pm \theta_2$. A change from addition to subtraction is very simply accomplished by interchanging two winding connections. The operation of a differential generator may be regarded as that of a synchro in which the rotor and stator can both be rotated. The field produced by the stator of the differential is similar to the one produced by the rotor of a synchro except that the field in the former can be rotated by changing the electrical input. The rotor of the differential, with its three windings acts like the stator of the ordinary synchro-generator and, of course, can also be rotated. The input and output of the differential, therefore, differ by an angle equal to the angular displacement of the shaft.

Synchro generators and motors are commonly used in aircraft navigational equipment to convey the angular position from various instruments to indicators in the cockpit. A synchro differential is generally met with in radio magnetic indicators which are instruments that indicate the magnetic North and the direction of a radio facility with respect to the heading of the aircraft, which is indicated by a fixed line ('Lubber line'). The instrument has two rotors, one of which carries the compass card and the other a pointer. The stator of the magnetic indicator gets its input from a synchro coupled to the gyro-compass. The stator of the radio indicator comes from a synchro associated with the appropriate radio facility. If the latter is a radio-compass, the input can come directly from the synchro coupled to the antenna system. But if a VOR is being used, the equipment gives the bearing of the facility with respect to North and to obtain the bearing with respect to the heading of the aircraft, the heading angle must be subtracted. Then the input to the radio indicator synchro is taken from a differential generator, as shown in Fig. III.4.

Resolvers. Resolvers are similar in construction to synchros, but the stator and rotor have two windings mutually at right angles (Fig. III.5). An input

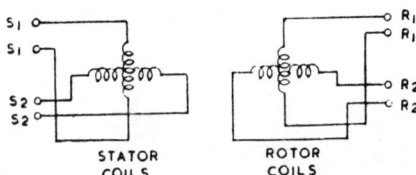

Fig. III.5 Schematic arrangement of a resolver

$E \cos \omega t$ to one of the stator windings induces voltages $E \cos \theta \cos \omega t$ and $E \sin\theta \sin\theta \cos \omega t$ in the two rotor windings, where θ is the angle between the plane of the primary and one of the secondaries. It thus resolves the vector into two components and hence its name. In instrumentation, resolvers are commonly used to bring about a phase shift of an ac voltage precisely related to the angular position of the resolver. If, for example, the phase of one of the rotor voltages is changed by 90° and it is added to the other rotor voltage, a phase change may be brought about, as is evident from the following relations.

Let $e_1 = E_s \cos \theta . \cos \omega t$ and $e_2 = E_s \sin \theta . \cos \omega t$ be the outputs of the two stator windings. Let the phase of the former be advanced by $\pi/4$ and that of the latter be retarded by $\pi/4$ by R-C networks, the relative amplitudes being maintained. If the resulting voltages are added, we get a voltage e_0 given by

$$e_0 = E_s \cos\theta.\cos (\omega t + \pi/4) + E_s \sin\theta \cos (\omega t - \pi/4)$$

But $\cos(\omega t - \pi/4) = \cos(\overline{\omega t + \pi/4} - \pi/2)$
$$= \sin(\omega t + \pi/4)$$

Substituting, $e = E . \cos(\omega t + \pi/4 - \theta)$

A phase change of $\pi/4 - \theta$ is thus brought about, which is equal to the angular displacement of the rotor plus a constant.

APPENDIX IV

A Functional Description of Navigational Facilities

THERE are many navigational facilities that are either in use or in the process of evaluation which it has not been possible to include in the main part. There are some facilities which are either obsolete or obsolescent but to which references are frequently made in literature. A brief description of some of these are included here. The facilities listed are arranged alphabetically.

BABS   This stands for 'beam approach beacon system'. This is a landing aid operating in conjunction with Rebecca interrogator in aircraft. It is a pulsed secondary radar beacon operating in a band at about 220 MHz. By lobeswitching techniques, it gives lateral guidance to aircraft (like the localizer) but has no facility for vertical guidance. But as distance information is available, the pilot can use it, along with the altimeter, to keep to the desired glide-slope. The earlier versions of Rebecca had a cathode-ray indication but this has been replaced by a right-left meter indication in the later models. BABS is not very accurate as a landing aid but is a useful addition to other facilities.

BLEU   The letters stand for 'blind landing experimental unit'. This is a blind landing system in which the lateral position of the aircraft is determined by sensing the magnetic fields set up by cables buried in the ground in the approach zone. Position in the vertical plane is determined by a radio altimeter. The facility is in the stage of development and operational testing.

CONSOL   This is the same as the system which was developed in Germany during the last war called Sonne. It is a rotating radio beacon operating in the LF/MF band which employs a system of three antennas producing a multi-lobed pattern which is switched to produce a number of equi-signal courses, as in a radio range. Off these courses, either a dot or a dash will predominate. As the pattern rotates slowly, the equi-signal courses also rotate and an observer can find his position within a lobe by counting the number of dots or dashes he receives before obtaining equal signals from both the patterns. This still leaves an ambiguity as there are about 20 lobes in the pattern but this can be resolved. Only a radio receiver is required in the craft to utilize this facility. Useful ranges of 1000 to 2000 km have been obtained with consol.

CONSOLAN   This is the same as consol except that a two antenna system is used instead of three-antenna one as in consol.

DECTRA   (Decca tracking and ranging) This is a long range hyperbolic navigational system working at a frequency of about 70 kHz. The system is designed to provide navigation information over a long route, particularly over the sea, as for example across the Atlantic. A master-slave pair is provided at each end of the route and the base line is so short that the hyperbolic lines are almost straight lines. The two pairs of stations help to give the lateral position. In addition, the frequencies of the two pairs are simply related and are phase-locked and comparison of the phase at the sub-harmonic gives a family of hyperbolae with a very long base line intersecting the former family and helps to fix the position of the craft along the route. A feature of Dectra is that the master and slave transmit alternately at the same frequency and a high stability oscillator synchronized to the master station is used for phase comparison.

DELRAC   (Decca long range area coverage) This is a very low frequency (10-14 kHz) hyperbolic system which is intended to give world-wide coverage. It is a CW system like Decca, but the transmissions of master and slave stations are made in time sequence and ambiguities are reduced by phase comparison at subharmonic frequencies. The facility is in the developmental stage.

DME   (Distance measuring equipment) This is a secondary radar system operating in the UHF band. See Chapter 5.

DMET   (Distance measuring equipment TACAN) This refers to the distance measuring part (secondary radar) of the TACAN equipment. The ground installation of DMET provides only distance information to airborne TACAN receiving equipment or DMET receiving equipment (i.e. bearing information is not available). The DMET ground beacon is generally installed with VOR to provide bearing to suitably equipped aircraft. The combination is called VOR/DMET.

GEE   This is a hyperbolic system developed during the war in Britain, at the same time as Loran was developed in the United States. It is a pulse system operating in the VHF band and was intended for short distance precision air-navigation.

GCA   (Ground controlled approach) See Chapter 6.

ILS   (Instrument landing system) See Chapter 6.

LORAN   (Standard, SS, LF and C) Loran (standard) or Loran-A and Loran-C have been dealt with in Chapter 4. S.S. Loran (skywave synchronized Loran) was used during the last war. It operated at the standard Loran frequency but had a base line of 1800 to 2500 km. Synchronization by ground wave is not possible for such a separation between stations and so skywave was used for this purpose and hence the name. The chain consisted of two pairs of stations, with the base lines intersecting at right angles. Errors up to 5 nm in fix were encountered. Due to the nature of the propagation, it could be used only at night.

LF Loran (low frequency Loran) was conceived during the war but its development was not completed. It was to operate at about 100 kHz and envisaged cycle matching. It is actually the precursor of Loran-C.

MARKER BEACONS   As the name indicates, these are radio beacons which are intended to mark some salient point. The three markers associated with the ILS have been mentioned in Chapter 6. These beacons operate in the VHF band (at 75 MHz) The outer marker has a fan-shaped beam and is sometimes called 'fan-marker'. The others have essentially conical beams. The inner marker is also called 'boundary marker'.

A marker called the Z-marker is used in conjunction with radio ranges. It has also a conical beam and is intended to give an indication to the aircraft when it passes over the radio range.

NAVAGLOBE   This is a long-range navigational aid operating in the band centred about 100 kHz which provides bearing information. The ground station has three antennas arranged in an equilateral triangle and power is fed to two of them at a time, cyclically, for 1/4 sec. During the last quarter-second a pair of antennas is energized, one with the normal carrier and the other with a frequency differing by 100 Hz. This last transmission helps to synchronize the receiver and identify the three other transmissions. The bearing is computed from the amplitude of the signals from the three antenna tower pairs.

NAVARHO   An integrated rho-theta system consisting of a Navaglobe and Facom. The former gives the bearing and the latter the distance. The distance information is obtained by phase-comparison of two signals, one from the ground station and the other generated in the aircraft. The phase difference gives the distance that the em wave has travelled from the transmitter, if the phases of two oscillators are suitably set initially. This method calls for a very high degree of stability of the oscillators both in the aircraft and on the ground (at least 1 in 10^9 for 12 hrs) but this can be achieved by modern techniques, particularly the atomic clock. The frequency of the facility being about 100 kHz, phase comparison leads to ambiguity, but this can be resolved by phase comparison at the modulation frequency of 100 Hz.

POPI   (Post office position indicator) This is a hyperbolic system with a very short base line which employs phase comparison to obtain bearing. The development of this was undertaken by the British Post Office but it does not appear to have been put to extensive operational evaluation.

Radio-Mailles or Radio Mesh   This is a navigation system developed in

France. It is a hyperbolic system in which the frequency of one station differs from that of the other slightly, so that the space pattern moves with a velocity which depends upon the difference in frequency. Position lines are derived from the number of equi-phase lines that pass the receiver in a given time.

RADUX This is a low frequency hyperbolic system operating at 40 kHz. The Omega system is a development of Radux, the main difference being in the frequencies used. In Radux, modulation frequencies of 200 Hz and 10 kHz are used, the first to reduce ambiguities and the second to provide a vernier.

Radio Sextant This is a sextant operating on the radio frequency emission of heavenly bodies, like a radio telescope. Some equipment working in the microwave band designed to receive the emission from the sun seems to have been built and tested. It could also be possibly used in conjunction with artificial satellites.

Rebecca-Eureka This is a war time development of secondary radar navigational aid, operating in the VHF band. This is a precursor of DME. The direction of a transponder beacon could be determined in the craft by the use of two antennas and lobe switching technique. It is now obsolete. Eureka was the ground based beacon equipment and Rebecca the airborne interrogator.

SHORAN (Short range navigation) This is a secondary radar system in which fix is obtained by the craft, which carries the interrogator, by simultaneously interrogating two ground beacons (transponders).

TACAN (Tactical air navigation) See Chapter 5.

VOR (VHF Omnirange) See Chapter 3.

VOR—DME (See DME)

VORTAC An installation consisting of VOR and TACAN at the same site.

Z-MARKER See under Markers.

QUESTIONS AND PROBLEMS

1. Show that the voltage induced in the loop when it is derived on the basis of the rate of change of magnetic flux linking the loop is the same as given in Eq. 2.4.

2. A loop antenna consists of 10 turns of wire. The loop is tuned and the output voltage is 100 times the induced voltage. It is required that the loop output be at least 100 μv when the field strength of the electromagnetic wave is 10 μv/m at the frequency of 300 kHz. Suggest suitable dimensions of a circular loop.

3. Why is a balanced modulator stage used in the radio-compass receiver? It has been stated in the text that the operation of the receiver is equivalent to that of one using coherent demodulation. Justify this.
   Show that the null opposite the correct one is a position of unstable equilibrium.

4. The automatic VHF direction finder described in Sec. 2.8(b) employs two selective amplifiers (or active filters). Discuss the effect of a slight mistuning of one of the filters.

5. Draw the phasor diagram as in Fig. 2.15(b) when an aircraft is approaching the direction finder from 30° East to North.

6. The VOR signal received by an aircraft consists of a carrier modulated by a 30 Hz sinusoid and also by a sinusoid of mean frequency of 9960 Hz. Taking the depth of modulation in each case as 30%, write down the expression for the received signal.

7. In the instrumentation part of the VOR receiver (Fig. 3.8), suggest suitable band-pass characteristics of the variable phase signal and the reference phase signal filters.

8. Referring to Fig. 2.9, let the signal arriving after reflection be 10% of the signal arriving directly and let $\phi_d = 60°$, $\phi_r = 120°$. Assuming that the reference phase signal is not affected by the combination of reflected and direct rays, and also assuming that the two carriers are in phase, calculate the error in the indication obtained.

9. In the Doppler VOR described in Sec. 3.5, the antenna in effect rotates at 30 revs/sec on the circumference of a circle of diameter 5λ. Show that this leads to frequency modulation of the received signal with a frequency deviation of about 480 Hz. Suppose the carrier frequency of the station is changed by 5%, keeping the antenna unaltered, would the operation of the receiver be affected?

10. Two LORAN-A stations, as shown in Fig. 4.1, are 200 km apart and an aircraft is 300 km from A (the master) and 200 km from B (the slave). The prf is 20 pulses/sec. The coding delay is 1333 μsec. What is the interval that elapses between the reception of a pulse from A and the next pulse from B?

11. Discuss the merits of the frequency band around 100 kHz for navigational aids with reference to (a) investment in antennas, (b) propagation characteristics, (c) ground-wave and sky-way signals, and (d) signal/noise ratio.

12. The Decca Mark VII receiver employs phase comparison at frequencies of 5f, 8f and 9f. Draw a possible block diagram of the receiver on the lines of the receiver configuration for fine-fixing shown in Fig. 4.10(a).

13. Why are the transmitted and received frequencies different in the Interrogator and Transponder beacon in DME?

14. Suppose 50 aircraft are interrogating a DME beacon, and of these 10 are in the search mode. How many response and filter pulses does the beacon transmit per second?

15. The bearing indicator of a TACAN receiver shows a bearing of 30° East of North. Draw the waveforms at the outputs of the 15 Hz and 135 Hz filters (in Fig. 5.7). Note that the zero of the reference sinusoids coincide with North. Assume there are no site errors.

16. The localizer gives two equisignal paths (XO and $X'O$ in Fig. 6.2) of which XO is the normal approach path. Can the pilot use the part $X'O$ to come to the runway? If so, how does he have to interpret the indicator readings?

17. The following indications appear on the cross-pointer indicator (Fig. 6.7) of an aircraft using ILS for approach and landing:
    i. The horizontal needle is above the horizontal line.
    ii. The vertical needle is to the left of the central vertical line.
    Indicate what action the pilot has to take.

18. A pilot descending along a glide-path finds the "fly-up" indication but when he flies up, the indicator needle goes further up. What interpretation should he put on this?

19. What is the purpose of the 'squeezable' waveguide in GCA? Explain how the beam position depends on the width of the waveguide.

20. Calculate the Doppler shift in each of the beams in a Doppler radar of the Janus-X type shown in Fig. 7.3(d), given $\alpha_0 = 60°$ $\theta_0 = 45°$, frequency of operation 9 GHz, and assuming that the aircraft is on level flight with a forward velocity of 500 km/hr and a drift velocity of 100 km/hr.

21. Develop equations similar to Eqs. 7.3 to 7.6 for the Janus-λ system of Fig. 7.3(c).

22. In the system shown in Fig. 7.3(b), suppose the forward velocity is obtained by subtracting the frequency of the beam 1 from that of the beam 3. What is the percent error in forward velocity if the antenna system tilts forward by 5°? Assume that the depression angle $\alpha = 60°$.

23. A gyro rotor has a mass of 0.3 kg and radius of gyration of 1.5 cms. It rotates at a speed of 12,900 rpm. Find at what rate it precesses when a torque of one kg-m is applied perpendicular to the spin axis.

24. Derive Eq. 8.8 from Eq. 8.7 and justify the expressions given in Eq. 8.9.

REFERENCES

1. BOWDITCH, N., *The New American Practical Navigator*, U. S. Hydrographic Office, Washington, 1964.

2. BOND, D. S., *Radio Direction Finders*, McGraw-Hill Book Co., New York, 1944.

3. KEEN, K., *Wireless Direction Finding*, Iliffe and Sons, London, 1947.

4. HOPKINS, H. G. and PRESSEY, B. G., "Current direction finding practice," *Proc. IEE*, Vol. **105** (B), Supp. 9, 307-316, 1958.

5. *Radio Research Special Report No. 22*, "Siting of direction-finding stations," Dept. of Scientific and Industrial Research, U.K., H.M.S.O. London.

6. TERMAN, F. E., *Radio Engineers Handbook*, Mc-Graw-Hill Book Co., New York, 1950.

7. CLEAVER, R. F., "Development of Single receiver automatic Adcock direction-finder for use in the frequency band 100-150 Mc/s, *J. Inst. Elect. Engr. London*, Vol. **94** (III), 783-797 (1947).

8. JOLIFFE, S.A.W., "Some factors in the design of VHF automatic direction finders," *The Marconi Review*, Vol. **22** (135), 168-198, 1959.

9. EARP, C. W. and GODFREY, R. M., "Radio direction finding by cyclical differential measurement of phase," *J. Inst. Elec. Engr. (London)*, Vol. **94** (IIIA), 705-721, 1947.

10. EARP, C. W. and COOPER-JONES, D. L., "The practical evolution of the commutated aerial direction finding system," *Proc. IEE (London)*, Pt B, Supp. 9, 317-325, March 1958.

11. LUNDBERG, F. T. and BUCHER, F. X., "The cage-type VHF phase-comparison radio range antenna," *Electrical Commun.*, Vol. **29**(2), 108-116, June 1952.

12. HURLEY, H C., ANDERSON, S. R., and KEARY, M. E., "The Civil Aeronautics Administration VHF omnirange," *Proc. IRE*, Vol. **39**(12), 1506-1520, Dec. 1951.

13. SANDRETTO, P. C., *Electronic Aviation Engineering*, IT & T Corp., New York, 1958.

14. BAUSS, W., *Radio Navigation Systems for Aviation and Maritime use*, Pergammon Press, Oxford, 1963.

15. STRONG, C. E., "General aspects of short-range Rho-Theta systems," *Proc. IEE*, Pt B, Supp. 9, 284-306, 1959.

16. THORNE, T. G., *Navigation Systems for Aircraft and Space Vehicles*, Pergammon Press, Oxford, 1962.

17. HANSFORD, R. F. (Ed.), *Radio Aids to Civil Aviation*, Heywood, London, 1960.

18. POWELL, C., "The Decca navigation system for ship and aircraft use," *Proc. IEE*, Pt B, Supp. 9, 225-234, 1958.

19. ROBERTS, G. E., "The design and development of Decca flightlog," *J. Brit. IRE.*, Vol. **12**, 117-131, 1952.

20. KEYTON, M. and FRIED, W., *Avionic Navigation Systems*, John Wiley, New York, 1969.

21. MOORCRAFT, G. J., "Precision approach radar," *J. Inst. Elect. Engr.*, **15**(B), Supp. 9, 344-350, 1958.

22. SKOLNIK, M. I., *Introduction to Radar Systems*, McGraw-Hill, New York, 1962.

23. TERMAN, F. E., *Electronic and Radio Engineering*, McGraw-Hill, New York, 1955.

24. McMAHON, F. A., "The AN/APN-81 Doppler navigation system," *IRE Trans.*, ANE-4, 202-211, Dec. 1957.

25. PITMAN, G. R. (Ed.), *Inertial Guidance*, John Wiley, New York, 1962.

26. SLATER, J. M., *Inertial Guidance Sensors*, Reinhold Publishing Co., New York, 1964.
27. SCARBOROUGH, J. B., *The Gyroscope—Theory and Applications*, Interscience Publishing Co., New York, 1958.
28. WRIGHLEY, W., HOLLISTER, W. M., and DENHARD, W. G., *Gyroscopic Theory, Design and Instrumentation*, The MIT Press, Cambridge (Mass.), 1969.
29. PARVIN, R. H., *Inertial Navigation*, D. Van Nostrand, New York, 1962.
30. KALMAN, R. E., and DECLARIS, N. (Ed), *Aspects of Network and Systems Theory*, Holt, Reinhart and Winston, 1971.
31. REINTJES, J. F. and COATE, G. T., *Principles of Radar*, McGraw-Hill, New York, 1952.

Index